THE POWER OF THE POSSIBLE

THE DIRE STATE OF INNER CITY EDUCATION AND ONE WOMAN'S REVOLUTION TO FIX IT

VALERIE GROTH MSW, MA

ISBN (PAPERBACK): 978-1-944878-65-8

First Edition

Jacket design: Colleen Keith

Dedicated to Ryan Banks, and the hundreds of other young victims of gun violence in Chicago.

The question is not whether we can afford to invest in our children. The question is whether we can afford not to.

—MARIAN WRIGHT EDELMAN

The people who are crazy enough to think they can change the world are the ones who do.

—STEVE JOBS

TABLE OF CONTENTS

INTRODUCTION

. . .

It had been a long school year, and I had been working long hours. So even having a low-key dinner out with friends and staying at a suburban hotel overnight with my boyfriend seemed like a great weekend away. In fact, my mini-vacation had left me feeling rejuvenated and ready to tackle the rest of the school year. Although my job as a social worker at two of Chicago's inner city schools had quickly shown me added dimensions of the word 'stress,' I'd remained focused on what my students most needed: my support and guidance as they navigated through countless challenges and traumatic events no child should have to endure. After a luxurious morning spent sleeping in on the last day of a quick overnight getaway, I'd put on the TV in our hotel room to check the weather and noticed the news ticker announcing that a young boy had been shot and killed near the school where I worked.

"Oh, no!" I blurted out to my boyfriend, John. "I hope it wasn't someone from my school!"

Given there were no other details, I focused on all of the work I had to do when I got home as we prepared to head back to the city.

As we were packing up our bags to leave, my phone rang, and I saw it was Dr. Leonard, the vice principal. I immediately thought, *It's odd for her to be calling me on a Sunday morning.* " Ms. Groth, one of our kids was shot and killed last night. It was Niazi Banks."

"Who?" I asked her to repeat the name, because I didn't know any students by that name.

"Niazi Ryan Banks."

I had forgotten Ryan's given name was Niazi. From that moment on, I didn't hear anything else she said. John told me later I screamed. I began to cry hysterically, so much so that someone from the hotel came to our door to see if everything was okay. Everything from that point became a blur.

I couldn't believe Ryan was dead. *Ryan...* the boy who'd tried (unsuccessfully) to teach me how to do the Dougie, a popular hip-hop dance move. *Ryan...* the kid who wouldn't hurt a flea. *Ryan...* one of the happiest, sweetest students who ever walked the halls of my school. *How could this have happened?* I knew many 12-year-old boys not only looked and acted like grown men, but were gang-involved and had already been in and out of the prison system. *But not Ryan.* He wasn't the seventh-grader with a mustache who looked like a 17-year-old; no, he was skinny and bird-like and truly still a kid.

No matter what kind of thinking or analyzing I did, I just couldn't understand how one of my favorite students was now gone . . . *shot dead.* So many things ran through my head, one of them being I hadn't even seen Ryan in what felt like forever. Sadly, because of my growing caseload, I hadn't been able to see him as regularly as I would have liked. Given Ryan was one of my more well-behaved students, I'd had to address so many other instances with those who were constantly fighting and misbehaving. I had also addressed back-to-back crises over the last month, and those situations obviously took precedence. To lose Ryan was unfathomable, but knowing I hadn't seen him recently made me even more devastated.

I knew there was nothing I could have done, but I felt terribly guilty I had been pulled into issues with other students who didn't want my help when there were kids like Ryan who wanted my support, but who didn't take precedence. I had always seen my work as a kind of triage system: there were kids who wanted my help, but didn't need it; kids who needed my help, but didn't want it; and kids who wanted my help *and* needed it. Like a triage unit, it always made the most sense to me that, since I couldn't possibly see all of the hundreds of kids in my school who fit into one of those three categories, my time would be best spent working with those who needed my help *and* who were also receptive to it.

In an ideal world, I wouldn't have to make that decision . . . but the world of CPS (Chicago Public Schools) was anything but ideal. The bulk of my time seemed to be sucked into issues where I wasn't able to be as impactful. That led to me having not seen Ryan for far too long. Now, it was too late.

? Niazi

? boyfriend

ONE

. . .

Arnold Math and Science Academy? I read with eyebrows raised. *That doesn't sound like an inner city school... it must be a magnet school for gifted students.* I had just received my placement for my second year Master of Social Work internship. While all of my peers in the MSW program had applied to suburban schools, I was the only one who had especially wanted to work in Chicago Public Schools, a district known for being one of the "worst" in the nation. I'd always assumed the reason for that stemmed from my upbringing. My parents had lived in Morocco for a few years while working in the Peace Corps in the early 80s, and I had grown up hearing about the sacrifices they'd made when they were there. It was very challenging for them living in a developing nation, but of course life was exponentially harder for the majority of the Moroccan citizens they interacted with who lived in conditions that would appall most Americans.

I'd been raised listening to stories about how my parents put a large rock in the fire and then wrapped it in newspaper to put

1

at the foot of their bed to keep them warm at night. They worked as a preschool director (my mom) and a welding teacher (my dad) for Moroccan students in classrooms that were barely more than four brick walls, with few resources to speak of. My father tells the story of how a man in the village where they lived once came to him in a state of panic, stressing that his goat was dying. The man begged my dad for help, assuming the two Americans in town had special resources and knowledge. My father patiently explained he was not a veterinarian, but agreed to go to the man's home to see the goat. When they arrived, it was clear to my dad what was wrong. The animal was starving—he was down to skin and bones. "Food was hard to come by," he'd tell me, "but the man was relieved to know there was at least a solution to the problem." My father was flabbergasted the man wasn't aware of this basic need that wasn't being met. Needless to say, the people in the village were often barely surviving.

When my parents returned to the U.S. after their stint in Morocco, they continued to give back to the community in other ways. Throughout my childhood, it was regularly impressed upon me how important it is to volunteer and to help others who are less fortunate. I'll admit, there were years of my young life when this didn't quite sink in, and for awhile I was more drawn to business pursuits and the lure of entrepreneurship.

But during college, I shifted my focus from business to psychology, and ended up being pulled toward a master's degree in Social Work. I had always loved being around the elderly, and my plan was to work in gerontology after finishing my degree. However, during my MSW program, it was emphasized if I ever wanted to work in a school, I had to complete an internship placement during my second year of the master's program—that is, it was now or never.

I didn't want to live with regrets, so I signed up for the school placement, assuming it wasn't a path I would actually end up taking long term. I *was* looking forward, though, to working with disadvantaged inner-city children and teens. It had deeply disturbed me that so many of my classmates had no interest in working with this population, and that made me even more compelled to do so.

So when I heard about my placement at Arnold (which I presumed to be a more "prestigious" public school), I was confused, partially disappointed, and, if I'm honest, a bit relieved. I thought, *Maybe this is a sign I'm not cut out for working in the rough inner city schools, and I'm being placed at this math and science academy for a reason.* Grad school was hard enough. I concluded, *Perhaps it's a good thing my placement school will be less stressful than I had anticipated.*

A few weeks later, I drove to Arnold Academy with nervous anticipation. At the time, I was living in Oak Park, Illinois, which is directly adjacent to the west side of Chicago. I was happy to hear my school placement was in the Austin neighborhood, not far from my apartment, a tiny, old college rental located in the safe, cushy center of Oak Park.

As I drove past Austin Street, which separates Chicago from Oak Park, I immediately entered a different world. The tree-lined streets seemed to disappear, replaced by abandoned storefronts and run-down buildings. My assumption had been wrong: the Austin neighborhood was poverty-stricken, and, from the looks of it, I was perhaps one of the only white people in this mostly African-American section of the city. Being a summer day and with my windows down, this juxtaposition was highlighted. I went from enjoying the sights and smells of blossoming trees to the sounds of a few men yelling "Hey, Snowflake!" and other cat-calls as I drove by.

I arrived at Arnold, an old building looking from the outside much like the schools I'd grown up attending in northwest Indiana. But once I was inside, the similarities ended. Stepping through the door, I was immediately hit by a wave of heaviness. The school felt dark, dingy and unkempt . . . and even more, it seemed forlorn, like it was giving up.

I took a deep breath and told the security guard who I was there to see. (*Security guard?* I wondered. *Maybe this isn't a magnet school after all.*) My new supervisor was called to the front desk to meet me. Monica was a doppelganger for Miranda Bailey of *Grey's Anatomy*, and I would soon learn this resemblance went past her outer appearances. Monica was full of love for her students, but, like Bailey, was tough as nails. Monica gave me a tour of the building, and I soon realized "Math and Science Academy" was a name that meant very little.

My assumption that Arnold was a magnet school was incorrect, and I was told most Chicago schools were given names like this. I understood the logic (or wish for a self-fulfilling prophecy): the moniker was selected in hopes that students would live up to the name of the school. While that theory made sense, it was also clear there were many other factors that made life challenging for students at Arnold.

As Monica debriefed me on the caseload of students I would be working with that year, I realized my job would involve so much more than providing therapy using the techniques and theories I'd learned in grad school. Clearly, these students needed so much more—many of them did not have their basic needs met. Monica spoke of Leslie, who was effectively mute, as a result of living in a horrific home environment, and Cardanisa, who was bounced around from foster home to foster home. There were students who were suicidal, and in and out of the psychiatric hospital—often because they were dealing with so many traumas at home. She also listed a significant number of students who were chronically in trouble for fighting and bad behavior.

After the tour concluded, we set up shop in a room in the basement of the building that housed the social worker, school psychologist and speech pathologist. All of these clinicians were obligated by law to provide one-on-one service to students who were on their caseload, and those who were providing therapy (Monica and I) were supposed to have a private space to do so. Because there wasn't enough office space to go around, our desks were located in this basement room . . . but Monica and I had to search the building for a secluded corner to take students in order to provide counseling services.

I was soon tasked with seeing students on my own, which meant providing individual or group services to those who had an IEP (Individualized Education Plan). I hadn't yet learned anything about group counseling in my master's program, so I focused on providing individual counseling. I would anxiously poke my head into a classroom to call a student's name and always got curious glances from the entire class.

I learned Arnold did have two Caucasian teachers, a married couple, but they were housed in a separate annex building dedicated to grades K-2. In other words, I was the only white person in the building, with the exception of the school psychologist, who was actually there just one day a week. Looking back, I realize I was quite naive about how to handle issues around racial diversity. I looked forward to working with my students, despite our different cultural backgrounds, but I hadn't realized they often were not as excited to see me.

It didn't take long to learn many students at the school had only interacted with white men and women for two reasons: they were either having to deal with white police officers or white social workers, both of which were usually very negative interactions. In fact, many of them were fearful of white people, with good reason. Their encounters had often been with white police officers who broke down the front door, handcuffed one or both of their parents and took them away to jail. For some children, white social workers came into their homes to take *them* away from their parents (often without explanation or at least, it seemed, to their young minds, without good reason or just cause).

TWO

• • •

State guidelines wanted social workers to spend more time with whole classrooms and less time with students one-on-one (thinking it's a more efficient use of our time). In my view, this was a misguided recommendation, as a great deal of students—in Chicago, the suburbs, and beyond—desperately needed support in a one-on-one setting. Students who were abused, neglected, or had witnessed violence simply could not be effectively supported in a classroom or even a small group setting. Nevertheless, this was what we were strongly encouraged to do by the social work department.

One of my first assignments from Monica was to work with Joey, a third-grade boy with a learning disability. Ostensibly, I was going to school to be trained as a therapist, but for this role I had to "push into" the classroom to help Joey with his reading. Part of my job was to assist him by reading passages he had trouble with so he would not be docked points for reading comprehension assignments simply because his reading wasn't up to grade level.

During a test one day, I read Joey a short story about a man who went from rags to riches. Students were then asked to choose which of the two following statements was fiction: a) An animal can talk, or b) A poor man can be happy. Joey matter-of-factly chose "b" as his answer, asserting out loud, "It's impossible to be happy when you're poor." In that moment, my heart broke for him, and I had my first glimpse into how standardized tests are biased against a certain demographic of student: those who've grown up with an expected set of resources and opportunities available to them.

After leaving Joey's classroom, I went to pick up Malcolm from his classroom. Malcolm was a slender, fourth-grade boy who never knew his parents and lived with his grandfather. He had been sent to school with shoes that were multiple sizes too large for him, so he was regularly picked on by other students for looking like a "clown." Malcolm was very reserved, and much of my time was spent gaining his trust by playing whatever game Malcolm chose that day, most often "UNO." For Malcolm, growing up in an abusive home where he often went hungry had led to his intense distrust of even those whose intentions were good. He had been let down by far too many adults in his life and was hesitant to allow himself to be hurt by another adult letting him down. However, after spending hours playing UNO with him and giving Malcolm the space he needed, he eventually let down his guard and began talking about his world with me.

I eventually found UNO was the surprising common denominator—"the great social equalizer"—by which I was accepted into the lives of many students over the years I spent in Chicago Public Schools (CPS). For countless students, trust was not something that came naturally, and many I worked with had either consciously or unconsciously put up a wall in order to protect themselves emotionally or physically or both. Though my master's program had only trained me in traditional therapeutic methodologies, I quickly learned I would sometimes have to adapt those methods while in CPS.

Many older students were unwilling to open up to me right away, and younger students were often unable to articulate their thoughts and feelings in a way that would allow them to benefit from traditional therapy models. But I wasn't going to be deterred and knew the amazing kids I was getting to know at Arnold needed me to step up my game in order to support them in the ways they so desperately needed. In between working at my practicum at Arnold and taking grad school classes, I scoured the internet for ideas. Amazon.com wasn't the mega-site it is now, but it contained a few resources that seemed applicable to the work I was doing. I ordered as many books as I could find on everything from art therapy to play therapy to how to conduct cognitive behavioral therapy with children.

One of the books I was excited to find was called *The Skin I'm In* by Sharon Flake. It profiles a seventh-grade African American girl and the challenges she faces around academic struggles, navigating the social hierarchy at her school, bullying and boys. At Monica's urging, I had set up a girls' group of seventh- and eighth-grade girls, and this book was just the thing to get them talking. The girls had never been presented with a book that articulated the issues they were facing so accurately, and they became more and more engaged as they enthusiastically took turns reading passages of the book aloud around the circle. We then discussed the themes that emerged from that day's reading, and lively discussions ensued.

Through these discussions, I began learning about the real struggles these girls were dealing with on a regular basis, about the trauma and hardship they were faced with when they left the school grounds. Many of them had dealt with chronic homelessness, and almost all of them had had an unstable living situation at some point in time. This meant anything from staying in a shelter to bouncing around from relative to relative, sleeping on couches, living room floors, and in hallways—sometimes with blankets and pillows, but often without either. The girls spoke about going hungry and about parents who'd chosen to purchase drugs in lieu of putting dinner on the table. They opened up about losing family members to gun violence or witnessing a close friend being shot to death in front of their very eyes.

And sometimes, they'd talk about being abused. A large chunk of my time in CPS was spent dealing with cases of students being abused or neglected at the hands of their guardian. I quickly learned the procedure to notify DCFS (the Department of Children and Family Services). While all school staff members are legally bound to report suspected child abuse or neglect, this responsibility almost always fell onto my lap or Monica's. Teachers are busy enough as it is, and there was also a high level of apprehension about the process.

I didn't mind being the person designated as a trusted source to make this call, but it was frustrating knowing so many suspected abuse and neglect cases seemed to go unreported. It was commonplace to have a teacher tell me about a suspected case weeks or even months after the fact, when a report should have been made immediately. It also was not as credible a case when I was the one to call DCFS (versus having the teacher call themselves), and yet some teachers refused to make the calls themselves.

I could understand their reluctance: calling DCFS was one of the responsibilities of my job I dreaded the most. It was my legal and ethical duty to report any suspected abuse or neglect, even if I didn't have the evidence to back it up. The job of a "mandated reporter," in other words, is just that: to report abuse. The job of DCFS workers is to investigate and to decide if the report is well-founded or not. (My belief is this policy would benefit from more stringent enforcement and consequences—if proof comes forward a teacher knew of abuse, but didn't call DCFS, legal and/or financial consequences should be levied.)

For me, the hardest part was knowing, no matter what, there was no good ending to the abuse-neglect equation . . . or so it seemed in the cases I was working. Children were very rarely removed from the home. It's a challenging dynamic for kids or teenagers who are removed without warning and then immediately placed with a relative or into a foster home. There are certainly some terrific foster parents in the world, but there are also those who take on the role for the paycheck. In fact, according to one social service agency[1]:

---

[1]   [https://www.childrenshomeandaid.org/facts-foster-care/]

- Each year, more than 300 children will enter the foster care system in Illinois *due to abuse or neglect.*

- There are more than 16,000 children in foster care in Illinois.

- In Chicago alone, there are more than 10,000 children and teenagers in the foster care system.

- Over 30% of foster children do not live with their brothers and sisters.

- 60% of foster children are in the bottom quarter of reading scores and 20% are older than their classroom peers.

Because the vast majority of DCFS calls I made while working in CPS) did not result in children being removed from the home, this meant one of two things happened:

1. After a DCFS worker went to the home to interview the parent and the child, on some occasions this would be the wake-up call for the parent to discontinue treating their child poorly. In some cases, the abuse was not a chronic situation, but rather a result of the parent being incredibly overwhelmed. Indeed, feeling overwhelmed is a recurring symptom of living in poverty, brought about by a combination of housing instability, not having ample food, and lacking basic necessities. Some of these include access to clean clothes and school supplies, as well as not having a high school or college education. One can add to this the fact that many of these parents were themselves victims of domestic violence. Throw in the often found factor of drug or alcohol abuse, and you have a perfect storm of incredible hopelessness, brought on by not seeing the light at the end of the tunnel. Without having been taught proper coping mechanisms, some parents resort to violence. In these cases, where the abuse was a one-time (or infrequent) occurrence, getting visited by a DCFS worker *could* be enough to stop the abuse or neglect in its tracks.

2. In other cases, however, a DCFS call to the home would unfortunately make things worse. More often than I can count, a child would report abuse to me or another school staff member, and, once DCFS was notified and investigated the situation, the student would come to school the next day with a black eye . . . along with a story corroborating the fact he or she got into trouble for reporting their parents to school authorities. As frustrating as these situations were, they were commonplace in an environment where the DCFS system was so flooded by reports they simply did not have the personnel to investigate as deeply as was often required. Further, I quickly learned there wasn't enough space in local foster homes to provide stable housing for students who truly were unsafe living in their home environment with a guardian who abused them.

In addition to the girls' group, I did my best to go above and beyond the typical roles and responsibilities of my job whenever I could. When it was national Eating Disorder Awareness Week, I made posters to display around the school that included hotline phone numbers to call for anyone who needed support with an eating disorder. However, I was immediately told by an administrator, "Black girls don't have eating disorders," despite evidence to the contrary. According to the National Eating Disorders Association, eating disorders are just as prevalent in women and girls of color. However, studies also show they are less likely to seek treatment (2016).

After beginning my work in CPS, I found that educators who go out of their way to provide exceptional service delivery were rarely lauded for doing so, but poorly performing teachers were seldom held accountable. In fact, at times I saw administrators bending over backward to accommodate poor teachers, at the expense of the best teachers, who were given extra responsibilities to overcompensate for those who weren't doing their job.

THREE

· · ·

Midway through my practicum year at Arnold, which was a K-8 school, I was additionally assigned to a public high school. Located on the far west side, Brewer High School was known for being one of the roughest schools in the city. As a short, small-statured woman who is often mistaken for being younger than my real age, I would be lying if I said I didn't feel intimidated as I first walked through the halls of Brewer. I was surrounded by high school students who were often much taller than me, and some of the high school boys looked like they were grown men in their 30s.

My supervisor at Brewer, Michael, was not only the school social worker, but he also doubled as the football coach. Though affable toward the students and seeming to be easy-going at first, Michael was quick to become strict when students weren't performing up to his expectations. His office was one of the go-to hangouts for many Brewer students, ranging from shy students who viewed it as their own safe space, to the football team who would hang out there during their breaks to discuss football plays..

Arnold was a tough school in its own right, and fights were commonplace there. But Brewer, which was actually comprised of four separate smaller high schools within one larger high school, was another beast altogether. The logic behind the segmentation was that smaller schools with their own principal and separate staff allowed for greater autonomy and the ability to create a more community-like, nurturing environment.

In an ideal situation where each school also had all of the resources they needed at their disposal, this would be a great plan. But Brewer was understaffed and under-resourced, and students were coming from one of the most poverty-stricken neighborhoods in the city. And with four separate schools under one roof, gang issues were a given. The principals and school security guards tried their best, but it's nearly impossible to control every single confrontation that happens within a school building, even with security cameras. At the time I worked there, Brewer was under investigation for a situation where a freshman boy was raped in the stairwell by older boys at the school. As tragic as that sounds, this type of occurrence was not an anomaly in many CPS high schools.

With the Brewer students being much older than those I was working with at Arnold, it was commonplace for students to have moved out of their parent's home because of abuse, a disagreement, being kicked out of the home for drug use or gang involvement, or because there simply weren't enough beds for everyone in the home or enough food on the table. As a result, a big part of Michael's role included being a quasi truant officer. While many districts have truancy officers, CPS had lost those positions due to funding issues.

Therefore, when a Brewer student had not attended school for weeks or even months, there was no one to enforce their school attendance, even if they were within the age limit of the law mandating such. It was commonplace for students to be out for months at a time, either with no explanation or with explanations that did not truly justify the absence: "I was taking care of my younger brother," "We went to go visit my grandmother in Florida," etc.

One day while talking to Michael, I asked him point-blank if he thought I would not be as 'relatable' to the students at Brewer because I was a young Caucasian woman who grew up in a comfortable suburban lifestyle in northwest Indiana. I wanted so desperately to help the students I was working with and did not want the cultural barrier to get in the way. But I knew many of the students at Arnold and Brewer had reservations about allowing me into their lives, an observation confirmed by the sideways glances I got on a regular basis.

Michael replied, "You don't have to get hit by a bus to know that it hurts."

His comment has stuck with me to this day. In that moment, I realized my deep sense of empathy and passion for seeing others succeed were more important than the fact that my skin was lacking in melanin.

This point was driven home by the end of the school year. I'd planned a field trip into the city for the students in my seventh and eighth grade girls' group. I had grown to adore the group, and not only had the girls grown closer to each other, but to me, as well. I wanted to do something special to commemorate the end of the year, and I felt making a special trip downtown with them would be a great way to celebrate.

Though Arnold is just a few short miles from downtown Chicago, most students in the Austin neighborhood rarely, if ever, left their neighborhood. It was commonplace for students to share with me they had never been downtown, save for perhaps a one-time trip to the Field Museum or Science and Industry Museum. I've found museums are a terrific means for both educating and inspiring students, and those in Chicago are some of the best in the world. But I knew so much of the value of visiting downtown Chicago was not just to attend an education-focused field trip to a museum, but for students to be exposed to the possibility and wonder of the city itself.

I firmly believe our environment is hugely impactful on how we feel about ourselves, how we relate to others, and how we see the world. Many of the children I worked with lived in dilapidated housing that was often lacking heat or air conditioning, and some were infested with cockroaches. The neighborhood they walked through to get to school had sidewalks full of trash and gangbangers at every corner. There were no real grocery stores with produce and healthy options; instead, food was purchased from the corner store that sold little more than liquor, chips and candy.

These children would then attend a school that felt dark and no more welcoming than a jail cell. It's no wonder children on the south and west sides of Chicago often have little self-esteem, lack drive for the future, and feel hopeless. Given that our environment reflects back to us our worth, the environment these kids were growing up in was shouting, "The world has given up on you!" To me, it was paramount to take these students out of their "normal" environment and open their eyes to some other possibilities.

When I was growing up as a young girl in northwestern Indiana, my family would go to Chicago for holidays, birthdays, and other big celebratory occasions. I loved the glitz and glamour of the city, and to me, the energy of downtown Chicago was palpable. Walking down Michigan Avenue, surrounded by local Chicagoans and tourists who had traveled the world to be on that famous street, I could practically *taste* the possibilities in store for me in this world. I loved the gorgeous parks, the lakefront, the stunning architecture, and the wide array of shops and restaurants. And yes, I wanted my students to experience *all* of this.

Since I was a grad student barely able to pay my rent at the time, I knew I didn't have the money to foot the bill for this trip on my own. I had to get creative, so I tracked down the phone numbers and email addresses for over 50 of the top restaurants in the city. I contacted all of them, explained what I had been doing with the girls' group and that I wanted to take them to a nice restaurant as a "thank you" for being such important participants in the group. Of all the restaurants I contacted, only one wrote back: Gibson's, which is one of the city's truly high-caliber steakhouses.

Thankfully, one was all I needed. Getting a school bus for a field trip, however, was a nearly impossible and surprisingly expensive endeavor, and it clearly wasn't cost-efficient to pay $800 for one school bus for a group of less than 10 students. Being in the Austin neighborhood, though, we were due west of downtown and therefore able to take the CTA's Green Line quite affordably.

When I told the girls about our upcoming trip, they were thrilled. We anxiously waited until we were told we had permission from the principal *and* from the area office, as many field trip ideas get nixed for one reason or another. No one from Arnold had ventured to take a group of students on the CTA with the intention to go to a nice restaurant, so without precedent being set, I was nervous about the proposal getting rejected.

FOUR

· · ·

Fortunately, our trip got approved and the day of our trip turned out to be one of the warmest days that spring. All of us—the girls, myself, Monica, and Ms. Campbell (the school counselor who helped us lead the group)—had had a long school year, but it had also been a brutally cold Chicago winter. Being outside in the warm weather was rejuvenating, and we gleefully set off for our downtown adventure.

Upon exiting the CTA station and climbing down the stairs from the "L" station to the sidewalk, it literally seemed we were entering a new world. When we'd first gotten on the Green Line, our group was departing from an impoverished neighborhood that felt as if the life had been sucked out of it years earlier, a place where entire blocks of boarded up buildings emanated sadness. Less than 20 minutes later, though, we were surrounded by the energy of bustling professionals headed to work and wide-eyed tourists who had come from around the planet to sightsee and explore the many attractions Chicago has to offer. It was an unmistakable shift in the energy of our environment that was evident to both the adults and teens in our group. The girls' faces lit up and their heads swiveled excitedly to the right and left as they took in the sights and sounds around them.

Our day started off by walking to Michigan Avenue and then south, until we arrived at Millennium Park. Most of the girls had never seen "Cloud Gate" (informally dubbed "The Bean"), the massive bean-shaped metal sculpture, whose magical reflective quality makes it a favorite among both tourists and locals alike. We took photos by the Bean and then walked back up Michigan Avenue to our next destination: Northwestern University.

In planning the trip, I knew there was inherent value in just taking the girls to see cultural and historic sites and that simply exposing them to another part of their city—and another way of living, for many Chicagoans—would be incredibly impactful. But since we were already in the city, I couldn't pass up the chance to take the girls on their first college visit. With the exception of some 'city colleges' (i.e., two-year community college programs), there are few true university campuses located downtown. Northwestern's main undergraduate and graduate campus is located north of Chicago in the suburb of Evanston, but Northwestern's law school and medical school are located smack-dab in the middle of the city.

We walked through the Streeterville neighborhood until we found the law school and began touring the building. The girls walked around with a mixture of excitement and a hint of nervousness, apparently feeling somewhat voyeuristic, as though spying into a world they had previously never known existed. This was the very first time any of them had visited a college campus, and until that moment their only exposure to college had been through watching movies and TV shows.

Entering into a law school building (with no set plan in mind), we stumbled into a lecture hall that was empty. The girls looked to us to see if they had permission to walk down to the front to sit in the seats, and we smiled and nodded with encouragement. Monica and I took photos of them sitting in this 158-year-old room that was once, and still is, one of the most stunning architectural wonders in the city. Somehow, I hoped this would be a moment the girls came back to over the next few years, serving as a reminder to them of their potential, that they, too, were capable of ending up as students in that lecture hall one day.

After the photo ops, we headed back toward our final destination, the restaurant. After making a quick stop at the Hershey store, we found ourselves in the Gold Coast, one of the wealthiest neighborhoods in the city. The Gold Coast is full of multi-million dollar homes, high-end designer boutiques, and five-star restaurants. As we walked by well-dressed men and women headed to lunch, yet again were the girls blown away, seeing a world where other people lived so differently than those from the world they knew.

When we arrived, the Gibson's maitre d' kindly walked us to our reserved table, and I shared with the girls the amount of our gift card. I then had them 'help' me figure out the math to discern how much each of us could spend, allowing also for tax and gratuity. A full order of porterhouse steak wasn't in the budget, but many of the girls—excited to try a fancy meal for the first time—opted to split an order with another girl at the table. Our meals were fantastic, both in taste and presentation, a fact all the girls appreciated immensely. They couldn't stop smiling and talking about how delicious the food was. For dessert, we ordered a few slices of the carrot cake, which was perhaps the tallest, largest piece of cake I've ever seen. Given this was a sort of "initiation" into the world of greater possibilities for these girls, I was deeply grateful the entire meal at Gibson's was utterly terrific.

Once the bill came, I shared with the waitress that I had a gift card I was planning to use. She took it with her and came back shortly, only to tell me the gift card was valid only at other restaurants within Gibson's Group—such as nearby Quartino or Hugo's Frog Bar—but not for the actual Gibson's restaurant! After an initial moment of panic, I politely explained the situation and the manager allowed us to use the gift card. Truly a close call!

After lunch, we headed back toward the train, exclaiming all the while what a wonderful day it had been. I had an interview later that afternoon for a school social worker position for the following school year, so I split up from the rest of the group and took a cab to Perspectives Charter School in the South Loop. Everyone else took the Green Line back to Arnold.

The interview that afternoon was my first interview—not just that year, but also my first ever interview for a "real" job. I had gone straight from my undergrad degree into graduate school without a break in between, and so the only interviews I had been on in the past were for summer jobs. I remember feeling incredibly nervous during my interview at Perspectives School and could sense the interviewer didn't find me to be her ideal candidate. She asked questions I didn't know how to answer, and I remember wondering why I didn't learn such things in graduate school. I was disappointed to feel this way, as Perspectives was a great school and it was a position I sincerely wanted at the time.

Nonetheless, I was glad to have gotten my first interview under my belt. Perspectives would have been great, but it was a charter school and all I truly wanted was to work for Chicago Public Schools—it didn't matter to me whether it was a charter school or a public school. Charter schools are a part of CPS, but also their own separate entity in many ways, and so they interviewed separately for each school social worker they hired.

On the flip side, Chicago Public Schools only interviewed once; if you got the job, you were assigned to one of the public schools in the city, but you did not have any choice in where you got placed. The great thing about this system was when you got hired by CPS as a school social worker, you were set. That is, if you didn't like your school assignments, you were stuck there for the time being, but you could always request a transfer the following year.

Teachers, however, were only hired by individual schools. If you found you didn't like your school, you were on your own to find a better option. This policy put more pressure on the interview process. I knew if I was hired by CPS, I would be "in the system" (which was desirable); but if I didn't get hired, I would have no chance of working in the only school district I truly wanted to work for.

By the time my interview was over, it was getting late in the afternoon and I didn't want to get back to my car after dark, since it was parked in the Arnold parking lot. Taking public transportation would have been friendlier to my grad school budget, but my safety came first. I took an expensive cab right from the south side out to the west side, where my car was the lone car still parked in the faculty parking lot. The cab driver politely waited until I got safely into my car, and I drove back home feeling extremely content after an amazing day.

FIVE

$\bullet\ \bullet\ \bullet$

At that point, the school year was almost over, and our girls' group only had a couple of sessions left. Much of our remaining time was spent talking about what the girls learned on the trip and what they loved most. I'll never forget one of the girls in the group telling me that over the course of the year, she had completely shifted what she thought about me.

She said the first time I came into her classroom, she made a snap judgment: "I thought you would be a snobby, uppity white woman, someone I'd never dare open up to. But over the time I've gotten to know you, I've realized I'd misjudged you. And I'm happy I've learned you're someone who's always been there because you truly cared."

While I felt honored to hear her say this, I knew there was probably some measure of accuracy to her initial assumption of me.

When I first started at Arnold, I felt unsure of myself and was incredibly nervous to jump into the work of being a school social worker, knowing I'd had little training. I'm sure the kids could read my fear and uncertainty in my face: hiding my emotions has never been one of my strong suits and my face is usually a telltale giveaway of how I'm feeling inside. I knew going forward I wanted to learn how to be in a situation where I was uncomfortable, while still being able to convey respect for my environment and to embody calmness in spite of any chaos. Little did I know how many chaotic situations I'd quickly be facing, all of which would give me on-the-spot training for handling the realities of students' lives in inner-city schools.

As the school year at Arnold ended, it also meant my second year of grad school was finished, as well. I had received my MSW diploma, passed the necessary examinations to receive my LSW (Licensed Social Worker certification) and also my Type 73 (to certify me to become a school social worker). I was now equipped with a bachelor's degree in psychology and a master's in social work: everything I needed to land a great social work job. Right? These qualifications, plus the fact I'd been one of the top-performing students in my class and our class's Vice President, should have been all I needed to find a fulfilling job with a decent salary.

The social work profession is known, with good reason, for being notoriously underpaying. Still, having an MSW degree *should* have significantly increased my salary. However, it was May of 2008, and the country was in the middle of the biggest recession in recent times. I had gotten engaged earlier that year, and so for the past few months, I'd been so engrossed in my studies, my work at Arnold, applying to new jobs, and planning a wedding, that I had spent very little time focusing on how the economic downturn was impacting the job market.

One thing I love about the MSW degree, compared to other mental health master's degrees (i.e., counseling or psychology), is that it's incredibly versatile. With an MSW, one is eligible to work in a hospital, adoption agency, government organization, drug rehabilitation facility, and more—plus, those who had their Type 73 (like me) could work in a school, as well. All of my classmates and I optimistically sent out resumes to jobs in all of these places, but the majority of our applications were to work in social service organizations, which unfortunately were the ones hardest hit by the recession.

After working at Arnold, I realized that, although I do love working with the elderly, I wanted to shift my focus to stay working in the schools. I interviewed with Chicago Public Schools but also threw my hat into the ring for social work jobs that were not in the schools. I soon realized organizations that would have jumped at the chance to hire me a year earlier not only didn't have the funds to hire new staff members, they were actually laying off employees right and left.

That summer, I went on some interviews, but the pickings were slim. One job offer I wanted to take was that of a program coordinator at a local Boys and Girls Club, which was an organization I thought very highly of. I knew from a friend who worked there that it was a great work environment, and I loved the idea of supporting an organization whose values I believed in so strongly. I was so excited when I got the job offer, but after I profusely thanked the woman with whom I had interviewed, she went on to say, "And the salary is $20,000." My jaw dropped.

This was for a full-time position, and I had a master's degree, yet I was being quoted a salary that, at the time, would have been more appropriate for someone with an associate's degree. Such a low number felt like a slap in the face, considering I had over twice that in student loan debt. Realistically, $20,000 would hardly be enough to get by in my hometown in Indiana, let alone while living in Chicago. As much as I had wanted the job at BBBS, I declined, believing I would be able to find another position that *at least* covered my basic living expenses.

As the summer went on, though, I started feeling nervous CPS wasn't going to hire me. I knew most school employees were hired right before the beginning of the school year, but with the recession looming over me, I didn't want to take any chances. I made a conscious decision to lower my standards and affirmed I would take the next job offer I found as a backup, knowing I could always keep sending out resumes while working.

My fiancé and I had discussed where we wanted to live, and Evanston, the suburb directly north of Chicago, was high on the list. In desperation, I looked up every social service agency in Evanston and meticulously plotted the whereabouts of each facility on a map of Evanston. Determined, I loaded up my car with resumes and drove to Evanston, prepared to spend the entire day driving around from point to point, dropping off my resumes as I went along. I was hoping the personal connection—being able to shake the hand of someone at each organization—would help my cause, compared to impersonally emailing an application, as I had done in the past.

As expected, most of the organizations simply weren't hiring. The one where I seemed to have the most luck was at a home health care agency. I spoke to a woman who said I came by at just the right time, that they were looking for someone to be their Director of Social Services.

Until then, they had only provided health care services, but now they wanted to expand to also offer counseling and case management services. The pay would be $40,000. Wow! To me, after being recently pitched an offer of $20,000, this felt like hitting the lottery. I would be financially better off and would get to have a pivotal part in starting a new arm of the organization from scratch. My inner entrepreneur loved this idea, and after also interviewing with the CEO of the company, I was offered and accepted the job.

I started work and soon realized the job was... well, not what I expected. I was given absolutely no guidelines about my role within the company or what I was supposed to be doing. The entire organization seemed incredibly disorganized, and the CEO changed her mind daily about what she wanted me to be working on.

Some of my days were spent driving around to low-income housing buildings to speak to elderly clients about what case management needs they had, such as food or counseling. If they needed food, my job was to wait in line at food pantries to get them food. Dressed professionally, I stuck out like a sore thumb in these lines, compared to the other people who were clearly homeless. I felt uncomfortable doing this duty, as I was constantly receiving side glances from both the homeless *and* the employees, who didn't know I was picking up food for someone else. The food pantries I went to didn't ask for identification or any type of proof you were truly in need. Anyone could come in and take food, no questions asked. I felt badly that some people probably thought I was taking advantage of the system.

Other days, the CEO of the company told everyone at work to stop what they were doing, and then asked us to engage in cultural rituals. The CEO seemed to place a lot of stock in traditions. These days would be spent having all of the employees watching her and a shaman walking around from room to room, blessing each corner of the building for prosperity. She believed the color red was lucky, and so on these days it was mandatory we come to work wearing red!

I soon realized the company wasn't a good fit for me; I felt like my role wasn't clearly delineated and when I asked questions, I was not given any answers. When I asked for the resources I needed to do my job, my request was deflected. So when I received a call on my way home from work one day from Veronica, one of the social work managers at CPS, I was elated. I was offered a role working on the south side of Chicago, which was exactly what I'd wanted!

Though it was the job of my dreams, it was still a big decision to make. Working for CPS meant I would have to live in Chicago in order to fulfill residency requirements, and Brad and I had been planning to live in the suburbs. I called him to discuss this dilemma, but he had just arrived in Las Vegas for his bachelor's party and I was told to "make the decision on my own." Frustrated at his lack of investment in this big decision, I called Veronica back and told her I would take the job.

SIX

. . .

Once Brad arrived back in Chicago, we quickly began to hunt for apartments in Chicago. We both wanted to buy a condo soon but didn't want to feel rushed into the decision (i.e., within the next week). Instead, we found a short-term apartment rental building and within days, we'd moved in. The following week, I started my job at Chicago Public Schools.

I had been assigned to two schools on the far south side of Chicago. Until that point, I was only familiar with the west side of Chicago and had never spent any time on the south side. My first school assignment was so far south, it was nearly in Indiana. In fact, my GPS wasn't working that day and I missed the exit for my school . . . and actually drove across the Indiana border before circling back to the school. It was a rainy day, and getting lost in the rain wasn't the best start to my new job. I eventually made it to Jonathan Language Academy just in time. After checking in at the main office, I was shown to my office which was essentially a large classroom that contained seven desks. This room was for the team of clinicians: the school nurse, social worker and psychologist, all of whom were stationed at multiple schools, as well as the case manager and the vice principal, who were there full-time.

I was given a brief tour of the school and then shown to the area where I was to see students. Since there was no privacy in the large office where my desk was located, and students were certainly entitled to privacy for counseling sessions, I wondered what kind of arrangements had been made for such. Instead of being taken to an empty office or classroom, I was shocked when the vice principal walked me through the gym and into the stairwell next to the stage. The stairwell was barely as big as a dining room table, and had poor lighting. But, that wasn't the worst of it. This already tight space was packed full with a piano and two industrial sized garbage cans—the kind kids dump their lunch trays into after lunch—with trash scattered around the floor. I immediately felt disheartened. *THIS was where the previous social worker met with students?!? There's hardly room for two people to stand up, let alone for me to be able to see students!*

Clearly, this dimly lit, dingy space wasn't even functional, let alone comfortable for students who were in need of counseling. *There's no way I'm going to ask students I'll be meeting for the first time to walk a significant distance with me, a stranger, and then expect them to open up while sitting in a space this unwelcoming.*

I took a deep breath and looked around me, ignoring for a moment the vice principal's presence. It would take some work, but I was committed to transforming what I was being given.

Knowing how impactful our physical environment is on our sense of identity and self-esteem, I knew that fixing up the space needed to be priority number one. As soon as I could, I drove to Indiana where my parents lived. On the way, I continued thinking, *the kids I'll be working with have enough on their plate without making them more uncomfortable.*

Once I arrived at my parents' home, I started gathering items from my childhood bedroom to bring back to my "office": a colorful lamp, a mini-Papasan chair, blankets and pillows, and decorations to put on the walls.

When I returned to school the next day, I sweet-talked the janitor into removing the piano and the trash cans from the room, which freed up the space immensely . . . but it still felt like "close quarters" to me. *But small can be cozy*, I thought, and I proceeded to redecorate the place with what I'd brought from Indiana. I set up the lamp in the corner and set the mini Papasan chair in the adjacent corner which left just a couple square feet of room left for me to place a colorful, checkered rug that was a remnant from my college dorm room. During my internship year, I had purchased books, therapeutic games, and art supplies, and I set up some bookshelves to store these items where the students could see them. There was just enough room left to squeeze in a few chairs, so I could have student groups, as well.

I also went to a teacher's supply store, where I loaded up on inspirational posters with motivational sayings, which I put up on the walls. In addition, I made some homemade signs of my own that contained some of my favorite quotes and expressions. When I was finished, the space looked completely renewed. It was by no means the ideal place to work with students, but it was *light-years* better than the way it was when I first saw it. As I was setting up my new space a couple students walked by and poked their head into the room, and they both gasped in wonder and asked if they could come back sometime to join me in the room. That was the goal—for students to feel comfortable and for the room to feel warm and inviting.

As a magnet school back in the 80s, Jonathan Language Academy students were admitted based on having high academic performance. Over time, though, the focus of the school shifted, and academic excellence was no longer a qualifying factor. However, it remained a 'magnet school,' which meant students still had to apply for admission. As a result, even though high test scores weren't part of the admission requirements anymore, most magnet schools attracted a different caliber of students.

Because it took a great deal more time and effort on the part of a student's parent or guardian to apply for a magnet school (compared to the neighborhood public school, where a child could be automatically enrolled in a matter of minutes), magnet schools typically attracted those who were more heavily invested in their child's education. This lead to magnet schools being comprised of students who were at least slightly more academically inclined or at least more academically motivated—coming from homes where education was highly valued—and typically were better behaved, as well. There would certainly be many exceptions to this rule, as I would soon learn, but overall my time at Jonathan would be a piece of cake compared to the trials I was faced with at my other assigned school, Thompson Elementary School.

As I followed Lake Shore Drive southbound and then weaved my way through the South Shore neighborhood, I noticed this part of the South Side was full of trees and buildings that, though old and often falling apart, I could tell used to be beautiful. This section seemed, in many ways, much more charming and at first glance, "safer" and more welcoming than what I was used to on the West Side, where I could drive for miles without seeing greenery of any kind. I later learned the reason for this stemmed from Polish and Italian immigrant families who made their homes on Chicago's South Side when they first arrived in America, before eventually moving to the north side of Chicago.

As I drove further south and east, I found Thompson Elementary was located in what felt like an isolated pocket of the city. It was just two blocks from the lake, but so far east it felt quite removed from the rest of the South Side. I would soon learn it was also situated in one of the most violent parts of Chicago, although it typically had less police presence than other notoriously rough South Side neighborhoods, such as Englewood or North Lawndale. In fact, this area of the city, known as The Bush neighborhood, was experiencing a great deal of gang activity, due to its having historically been mostly Latino until recent years, when more African American families had moved into the neighborhood. With those migrations came turf wars—local battles for territory between multiple gangs—and as a result, violent interactions between the rival gangs. The prevailing violence also engendered a "food desert" (no real grocery stores for miles), leaving few options other than run-down quick-stops that sold alcohol, snacks and soda pop.

At the time I worked there, Thompson was a fairly new school, so in many ways it stood in stark contrast to Jonathan. According to what I heard from a number of teachers and parents, the school was built not for the neighborhood children, but rather for the white kids who would attend at a future date, once the lakefront properties were built up. In other words, given the neighborhood was adjacent to the lakefront, it would (presumably) eventually be gentrified, with the most likely transition being to an upper class neighborhood.

As I walked in, I couldn't miss noticing the new building was quite large and also very bright with great lighting, which I hoped was a good sign. My "office" at Thompson was a room I'd be sharing with other clinicians, but as there was much more space to go around, I was glad to only have to share with two other staff members. I was told to see students in the annex of the library, which was a tiny and cramped space full of computers. It wasn't ideal, either, but at least it was free of pianos and garbage cans!

Though Thompson was indeed housed in a glossy, good-looking building, it soon became apparent the "insides" were full of challenges. During my first week on the job, I was in the middle of a meeting when I was called to the office—this was the first of literally hundreds of times I would hear my name being paged over the intercom over the next few years, each one being a call for me to address a crisis waiting in the main office.

When I got there, I was notified by the vice principal that a third grade student, Brady, was acting out in class and talking about wanting to kill himself. While panicking inwardly, I tried to maintain my composure on the outside. I thought, *a third grader threatening suicide? What have I gotten myself into?!* I went to meet the student who was on my assigned caseload. I introduced myself to Brady and we went to "my room" to talk.

Though I had never dealt with a suicidal student on my own before, I had learned at my internship how to handle the situation. I asked Brady a series of questions to determine the level of severity

31

of his threat to harm himself, whether he had a plan to actually do it, what his plan entailed, etc. Based on how a student responds to these questions, I would take one of three courses of action:

1. If I deemed the suicidal threat to be made in error or in "jest" (e.g., a child who accidentally blurts out, "Ahhh, I could kill myself!" during a hard test question, but used that as more of an expression of frustration, rather than an actual statement of suicidal ideation), the lowest level of response would be notify the parent about the threat— even if it was deemed to be harmless—and to have them sign a document notifying them about the situation and containing information about how to get counseling for their child, *if* they ever find themselves in a situation where it's warranted.

2. The second and third options both involve calling SASS (Screening, Assessment and Support Services), a hotline for ensuring student safety. If a child's parents or guardian had private insurance, I would call the insurance company instead of SASS (which was the government conduit for addressing the needs of low-income children whose families received public assistance). I would explain the situation to the intake worker who would then send an SASS-trained specialist to the school to meet with the student and me. They would ask the student similar questions to those I'd asked in order to determine if the student could benefit from outside counseling or if they needed immediate psychiatric hospitalization.

After asking Brady these questions, it was evident his suicidal questions warranted an SASS call, but in the moment I felt completely panicked about what to do next. *Do I call his parent? Do I tell the principal? Both of these seem important, so in what order do I do them?* Even worse, it was nearly the end of the school day and I knew I was running out of time. I stepped into the hallway, hoping to see the school psychologist, who I could ask for help. Instead, I spotted the speech pathologist, Heather. I explained the situation to her in a state of visible distress, but it immediately became clear this was not her area of expertise.

"Good luck, you'll be fine!!" Heather said, as she ran off to her next meeting.

I did my best to calm down so I could better handle the situation, although inwardly I was having a hard time not freaking out. I could not send Brady home by himself, but I also knew he would not be happy about staying after school. I remembered he had an older sister and notified the main office to call her to say Brady would be staying late, so she shouldn't worry. Two hours after the school day ended, Brady's mother and the SASS worker arrived and it was determined—based on the intensity of his suicidal thoughts—Brady would indeed benefit from immediate psychiatric hospitalization.

When the SASS worker told Brady about the recommendation, he started to mutter under his breath and paced around the room. He wasn't happy about having to go to the hospital, but in this case, he didn't have a choice. Brady's mother was able to maintain her composure and did her best to keep Brady calm.

Many hours after everyone else had left the school, I finally finished completing my paperwork from the event and found I was the last person in the building, aside from the janitor. It was now dark out and he offered to walk me to my car—the last one left in the parking lot—as it was not a safe neighborhood to walk around in after dark. By the time I got home, I was utterly exhausted, but presumed that dealing with a suicidal student would be an anomaly I wouldn't have to face on a regular basis. Little did I know, I would have four more suicidal cases that week, *at that school alone.*

SEVEN

· · ·

My first year was rough, to put it lightly. Yes, I had a Master of Social Work (MSW) certification, and I'd spent a year working at Arnold and Brewer during my internship. I quickly realized how completely unprepared I was for the job. The "work" we did during my MSW program was all theory, and we spent little time learning how to apply those theoretical concepts and philosophies to real-life scenarios.

My internship had exposed me to the inner workings of a CPS school, but I realized I'd only seen the tip of the iceberg. Monica had given me some students to work with and brought me to the occasional meeting here and there, but that was a minute fraction of the job responsibilities of being a school social worker. I felt as if I had been thrown into the lion's den and was on the verge of being eaten alive. And although these were my true sentiments at the time, this was still my dream job—I loved the kids, and loved the work—and I knew I had to stick it out.

At Thompson, I eventually became friends with Heather, the speech pathologist, and also Lauren, the school psychologist. A month into the school year, I had gotten married and taken a honeymoon to Mexico, and I returned just in time for Halloween. Heather, Lauren and I sat in the tiny annex room by the library and snacked on the treats we had brought to host our own mini-Halloween party. In celebration of Halloween, my wedding, and the fact we had survived two months of the school year, we dunked Cheetos into Nutella—devouring junk food was a favorite coping skill amongst stressed-out CPS staff—and shared stories about the crazy goings-on we had recently witnessed.

The tales ranged from a parent who'd flipped over a desk in a fit of rage after he didn't get his way during a meeting, to a student punching his teacher and then pulling down his pants in front of the class, and various other detailed accounts in between.

It didn't take me long to learn Thompson was going to be exponentially more challenging than Jonathan, which I would think of as my "easy" school in comparison, my breath of fresh air. At Jonathan, I had implemented a "Problems Box" in each classroom, and had explained to the children in each class that if they had any questions for me or another adult, or if there was something they wanted to talk about, they could put a note with their problem and their name on it into the box, and I would then come to talk with them about it.

The Jonathan principal thought it was a silly idea at first, but allowed me to do it anyway. It was a great way for me to get to know more of the students at my new school, but what I'd initially surmised turned out to be true: Jonathan School's "problems" paled in comparison to the issues for kids from Thompson. At Jonathan, problems included a sibling not sharing their toys at home, or a student being unusually nervous for an upcoming test. For a child, these are legitimate concerns and I was more than happy to work with these students to provide counseling. However, it was rare to experience an issue that was life-threatening.

Occasionally, there were exceptions to this rule. Not long into the school year, I was at a training (away from the schools) when

I got a call from the principal at Jonathan. I was told the mother of one of our first-grade students had been shot and killed by the father. When anything of that magnitude happened, my job was to drop whatever I was doing in order to attend to the needs of the crisis at hand. I left my training, headed to the school, and went to work. The boy whose mother was killed was not in school that day, but most of Jonathan's kids lived in the neighborhood, and word had gotten around quickly.

I entered the class to find dozens of crying kids. I said a few words to the class, conveying the entire school staff's sorrow and condolences regarding Tyrell's loss. I also told them I and other staff members were there to help anyone who needed to talk. I passed out construction paper and markers and told the class that anyone who wanted to could make cards to give to Tyrell to welcome him back to school when he returned. Eventually, I allowed the teacher to take over my "group leader" role so I could counsel individual students who appeared especially inconsolable and clearly needed counseling.

Back at Thompson, dealing with crises had become a standard part of my job. Hardly a day went by when I wasn't making an SASS call for a child who was suicidal or a DCFS call to report suspected child abuse or neglect. Not only were these situations tragic for the students involved, but these crises meant it was incredibly challenging to take care of the rest of my job.

A school social worker's main role is to provide services for students who have an IEP (Individualized Education Plan) that dictates they need to receive counseling. And I say the "main" part of my job because these services were the only work I did that would eventually be billed to the state of Illinois and for which Chicago Public Schools would be compensated for my time. Though there were hundreds of students in my schools without IEPs who also were in dire need of time with a social worker, it was ingrained in us by the social work department that our IEP students should come first, always.

However, whenever there was a crisis, handling that took precedence. Unfortunately, the frequency of crises at Thompson meant it was extremely challenging to see the students on my caseload, let alone the general education students (those without an IEP) who wanted and needed to see me, as well.

The fact is, I've worked with so many suicidal students over the years, I have lost track of most of their names. But there are many whose stories I will never forget, as long as I live. One memorable student was LaToya, who was suicidal and also schizophrenic. She believed she was the singer Nikki Minaj and would call my voicemail leaving me messages as though she was actually Nikki Minaj. LaToya was only at my school for two years, but she was also perpetually suicidal and in and out of the psychiatric ward. Her mom was a young mother who struggled with schizophrenia herself, and so LaToya lacked a solid support system at home to help her cope with her challenges. The year after she left Thompson to attend another school, LaToya got pregnant. The last time I heard about her, she was 16 years old and expecting her second child.

Rachelle and Nancy were two students who were also sisters, and I worked closely with both of them. They were a year apart and both incredibly bright students: either girl could have been Ivy League-bound. However, they were both chronically suicidal as a result of the trauma that was happening in their home environments. Both girls had been bounced back and forth between their parents, who were no longer together, and their mother suffered from both mental health and medical issues that left her in pain and often bedridden. She also had a young son from a different father, and he, too, suffered from a number of health issues which took up a lot of the mother's time.

This situation at home left the girls feeling unloved and emotionally neglected, but it turns out that was the least of it. Rachelle and Nancy both dealt with physical and emotional abuse at the hands of their parents, and both were also sexually abused by other adults who were in and out of the home. As a result, they both began to self-injure or "cut," using any sharp object they could find—from a knife to a pencil—to slice open their arms, legs or stomach. The cutting wasn't enough to stop the pain, though, and they both became so suicidal they were often in and out of the psychiatric hospital as often as twice a month.

These girls would experience some temporary relief from their emotional pain when they were safe at the hospital, only to relapse as soon as they were back in their abusive home. Whenever we had to go to the hospital, the hardest part was finding a parent to come meet us there . . . because neither of them wanted to go. The mother would audibly sigh and tell me she couldn't deal with this anymore and to call their father, who would say the same thing. One day, her father told Nancy, "Just fucking kill yourself next time, so I don't have to deal with you anymore."

As one can imagine, neither of these girls would ever actually end up in an Ivy League school. I spent literally hundreds of hours working with them, and sometimes the art therapy we did together—such as decorating coffee mugs with positive, inspirational phrases on them as reminders of their worth and value—would allow us to see a little bit of progress. But then, they would go home for the weekend and come back to school re-traumatized.

Rachelle and Nancy became more and more disconnected from school and from others and identified so much with their cutting and suicidal ideation that this became all-consuming. They both stopped caring about school and instead joined online chat rooms with other suicidal kids whom they had never met, trying to find community and love in strangers who understood them, since they weren't receiving love at home.

These two girls had such a high level of need, it was clear they both needed daily counseling. Nonetheless, in the prevailing CPS environment, that could never happen. As a result, I knew these girls had a very slim chance of even making it through high school without dropping out of school, becoming pregnant, or worse, having one of their suicide attempts end a once-promising life. Time passed and the day came when I realized neither Rachelle orNancy were in school any longer, and I would never learn of what became of them.

EIGHT

· · ·

I had gone into social work because I wanted to help people, I wanted to make a difference . . . I wanted to do my part to make the world a better place. However, I became increasingly frustrated with the dire level of need I saw around me and how there were just not enough resources to go around. I was assigned to two schools full-time, plus, from time to time, I would get asked to cover a third school. Counting all of those students among the schools I was asked to cover at once meant that I was one social worker for around 1,000 students.

According to the National Association for School Social Workers, most schools should have a ratio no less than one social worker to 250 students. What this means is a school in a district with ample resources and a high level of economic prosperity will have, at the *very minimum*, a ratio of 1:250. For a school serving the demographic of students *I* was working with—economically disadvantaged youth—the recommended ratio was 1:40. To compare, my 1:1,000 ratio meant that we needed *twenty five times* more social workers in order to comply with national standards.

Though my intention was to make a difference, it was rare when I actually felt I was doing so. There was so much need at each of these schools, particularly at Thompson, it felt like I was putting out fires right and left, but never actually making a deep impact in the lives of any of the students. There were so many crises on a regular basis, it was challenging enough to see the students on my caseload, let alone the general education students who waited outside my office door, hanging around hoping I would have a spare minute to see them.

It was commonplace for me to be working with a student who was in the middle of a crisis (e.g., a suicidal student, which meant I was required to drop everything I was doing for the rest of the day to attend to their needs), only to find I'd been paged to go to the office, where I had *another* crisis awaiting me. In those moments, I would find myself in the situation of having to bring Crying, Distressed Student in Crisis #1 with me down the hallway on the second floor and to the main office, so I could pick up Crying, Distressed Student in Crisis #2 who was waiting for me there. Because I needed to give Student #2 privacy, I would have to find another adult to watch Student #1; I couldn't leave a suicidal student alone, even for a second.

This was immensely trickier than it sounds, as every adult in the building was busy, and it was often impossible to find someone willing to watch any of my distressed students. In the cases where I *did* find someone, it was not uncommon for me to return from working with Student #2 to find the adult had left Student #1, *despite* my pleas to never let them out of their sight. I took suicidal ideation cases very seriously and tried to ensure a student in that state was never unsupervised, even for a moment, until we could get them the proper psychiatric support they needed.

In this generalized example (which specifically happened more times than I could count in my tenure working at CPS), after privately assessing the situation with Student #2, I would take both students with me upstairs back to my office. The hardest part about this was that, in doing so, we would walk by numerous classrooms. Students in their classes would see me walking by, run out of their class and yell my name: "Ms. Groth, Ms. Groth, I have to see you now!! Please, Ms. Groth!!" Many of them would go so far as to hang on my arm and try to follow me and Students #1 and 2 down the hall to my office. In those moments, I felt like I was in the middle of a war zone. There were *so* many students who were going through so much trauma in their lives, who desperately needed someone to provide them with counseling, who needed someone to listen to them, to love and support them. Looking back years later, I often flash back to these moments of my students hanging on me, crying out for help, and I'm often moved to tears thinking about the level of intense need they ha, and the fact that I'm no longer there to help.

These regularly occurring scenarios, at times, made me question the work I was doing. I knew I was good at my job and doing the very best I could under difficult circumstances. But more often than I would have liked, I wondered whether or not anything I was doing was making even a minute difference. Many days, as I drove home, I felt as ifI hadn't done enough that day. If I'd seen three students, I felt badly I hadn't see four. If I saw fourteen students that day, I felt badly I hadn't seen fifteen. It didn't take me long to realize there were wide-reaching system issues at play, which were getting in the way of my students being able to learn and achieve academically, as well as factors outside of the school environment that impeded their ability to live safe, secure and healthy lives.

Nearly every child at Thompson (slightly less at Jonathan) was living in poverty, and many also dealt with homelessness and chronic hunger on a regular basis. Still others witnessed violence at home or in the neighborhood. Students as young as five years old described walking by dead bodies in the street or in the hallways of their apartment building, as if it was no big deal. Others talked about walking to school down streets strewn with empty beer cans and drug needles (many streets didn't even have sidewalks). Countless students were victims of abuse or neglect. And, I could go on: Only 14% of CPS 9th graders complete college by their

25th birthday and within five years, the typical CPS school loses over half its teachers (consortium.uchicago.edu, 2014). Statistics like these make it easy for one to imagine the painful, ugly truths my students were conveying to me, over and over, day after day, year in and year out.

By my estimates, there were hundreds of students at each of my schools who were in dire need of additional resources they weren't being provided. There were so many students exposed to significant trauma outside the school environment, and yet here we were asking them to come to school and behave and perform well academically, despite the horrific environments they had just left and would soon return home to.

When we send our soldiers to battle in the armed services, many unfortunately come back with PTSD as a result of experiencing or witnessing horrific acts of violence. Thankfully, the majority of Americans have an immense amount of respect for our military men and women, and when they return from combat, we respectfully provide them with as many resources we can to assist them with healing and returning back the community in a positive manner. Typically, for both those who have suffered greatly and those who have been more fortunate, we honor them with well-earned living assistance programs, awards, medals, and even parades.

While those men and women earned and deserve every bit of those accolades, there are thousands of children across Chicago who have also witnessed heinous acts of violence, on top of often being hungry, homeless and exposed to recurring abuse or traumatic events. Yet in the thousands upon thousands of cases of Chicago's Southside public school students, they do not get even the bare minimum, let alone the proper amount of support and assistance they truly deserve. And awards or a parade? No, we *expect* them to learn. We *expect* them to somehow rise above their so often thoroughly toxic environments, though we have given them few-erresources and less support than we give to children and adults who have never been faced with such difficult circumstances.

It seemed incredibly unfair and unjust that I was able to reach the level of personal and professional success I had attained largely because I'd grown up in a secure, loving home in a safe neighborhood—and I had attended a school where all of my classmates had come from similar families and neighborhoods. In the community where I grew up, it was a given that everyone would go to college, and it was odd for a fellow student to decide not to. I was also surrounded by dozens of adults who were well-educated and successful.

However, I also remember stopping to take stock (during my time working at CPS), thinking back about how I was as a kid. At thirteen years old, I was well-behaved and a good student . . . mostly because that was what was expected of me, and I didn't know any differently. At the time, I had low self-esteem, and had I grown up in an environment similar to what my students had experienced living in poverty on Chicago's South Side, I felt certain I would have made different choices. It was clear to me, if I'd lived in that different environment during my early teen years, I could easily have fallen into making bad decisions: dropping out of school, getting pregnant, using drugs or joining a gang out of a need for validation, identity and acceptance.

I eventually became sick and tired of seeing so many students showing two or three "baby steps" of progress after working with me during the course of the school week, only to have them go home for the weekend and come back on Monday, literally ten steps behind. Mondays and Fridays were usually the hardest days of the week: on Mondays, students came back from being at home over the weekend, where they often went hungry or maybe even abused. Fridays were equally hard, with many students acting out behaviorally, which I recognized as a subconscious crying out for someone *not* to send them home. The same thing would happen before and after a long break. While a two-week Christmas vacation was a happy time of year for students living in healthy families and having a roof over their heads, for students who were homeless or living in unsafe families, two weeks away from school was often an absolute nightmare.

It didn't take long for me to decide enough was enough, and there *must* be a better way. I had only been working at my new job for a couple months when an idea popped into my head. Clearly (at least to me), Chicago needed a boarding school for inner city students, where they could get a great education in a 24/7 living environment in which they could feel loved, safe and accepted. *Eureka!* This idea seemed so obvious of a solution, I couldn't figure out why there wasn't already one in existence!

As I started to research the idea, I realized I wasn't the first person to have this idea of building a boarding school for Chicago's inner city students. In fact, at that time, Arne Duncan, the presiding Chicago Public Schools CEO, had been an outspoken advocate for urban boarding schools for years. (Duncan left his role as CEO the following year to become the U.S. Secretary of Education). I was so excited to read about Duncan's fervor for boarding schools, and temporarily, discovering this abated my impulse to proceed further. I felt glad Mr. Duncan would tackle this massive problem, and even though I felt it should have been addressed a decade earlier, I remember thinking, *If for some reason Arne doesn't follow through with his plan for a Chicago boarding school, perhaps I'll tackle it myself one day.* (Granted, in my mind I probably was leaning toward doing so when I retired or had boatloads of free time and extra money sitting around burning a hole in my pocket.)

NINE

. . .

Over the course of my first year at CPS, I dug in and dedicated myself further and further to helping my students, spending more and more of my time, energy and money to do so. As a newlywed, I should have been excited to rush home at the end of the day to see my new husband. And, I was . . . on the days when I had the luxury to actually leave work when the school bell rang. A much more typical scenario involved me staying hours after everyone else had gone home for the day, finishing up the paperwork I would have liked to have been able to complete during school hours (but couldn't, because I had spent the day addressing additional crises, as was usually the case) or making phone calls to parents.

This last duty was a grind unto itself, because the parents of the students I worked with were commonly living in the depths of poverty and thus, most could not afford to pay their phone bill each month—which meant their phone numbers changed or were disconnected often, sometimes on a weekly basis. It was therefore nearly impossible to get in touch with parents when I needed to, which posed a problem for a multitude of reasons. On the most basic level, it's incredibly important for school staff to be able to have regular communication with parents about how a student is doing academically, socially and behaviorally. My job routinely entailed needing to be able to relay messages to parents about a child who had gotten into a fight during school that day, or to tell them about a student who was found crying in the bathroom after being bullied.

I also needed to speak with them about strategies and techniques they could use at home that would help address the issues I was working on with their child at school. Their learning how to assist their child would decrease the likelihood that I was teaching the child one thing at school, only to have their parent be reinforcing the opposite behavior at home. Unfortunately, such educational/informational types of communications rarely happened, because touching base with parents via telephone was generally so unreliable.

But even more pressing were the phone calls I needed to make about students who had not been in school that day, in order to make sure they hadn't skipped school or run away, or calls to notify a parent that I was concerned their child was engaging in genuinely risky behavior. I also stayed after school making numerous calls to social service agencies, trying to find resources and services to support the needs of my students and their families. The process of accessing social services regularly proved incredibly frustrating, and I often spent long amounts of time on hold, only to be hung up on, sometimes after waiting for over an hour.

Far more often than I could count, phone calls made to government-run organizations would ring and ring endlessly, and nobody would answer, despite my calling for days on end. I wanted to rip my hair out just trying to find basic services for the families I worked with, to make sure they had food, shelter and clothing. And sometimes, trying to make my way through "the system" to find the right person to talk with seemed more like maneuvering through a labyrinth or a maze than making simple contact with a governmental agency established to help people.

The bottom line, as far as my post-newlywed life was concerned? Getting home late swiftly became the new normal. Also, exercise had always been important to me and after starting my work with CPS, I tried my best to fit in a quick trip to the gym at the end of each day. However, I found exercise was increasingly hard to prioritize when I'd come home so burned out after each emotionally taxing day—which seemed to be Monday through Friday most every week. In comparison, though, I felt deeply grateful to at least have access to—and be able to afford—a gym. I knew all too well what such a luxury that would be for the average South Side resident.

And you know, it seems easy for a celebrity trainer like Jillian Michael to spout off about how "there's no excuse for everyone with two legs to exercise, because anyone can go for a walk." The fact she is missing or ignoring is this: for kids and their families living in Chicago's South Side (especially in the violent neighborhood where Thompson was located), it would have been incredibly unsafe for anyone to go on a walk or a run for exercise around the neighborhood. Sure, plenty of people walked places on the South Side—without cars or the income to afford a Chicago Transit Authority pass to more easily get around, so walking was the main mode of transportation for most. But walking was something residents did only when necessary—to go to the store to buy food, for example—and time spent outdoors was limited as a result of the high possibility of violence erupting at any given time.

Indeed, it was common for students as young as kindergarteners to tell me stories about how they'd be playing at the park after school (while it was still light out), only to have to duck to the ground when they heard shots ring out close by. With gunfire an imminent danger at every turn, walking or jogging for exercise was just not prudent.

There were a handful of YMCA's on the South Side, but for the most part, most neighborhoods lacked access to a gym. And again, even walking from one's home to the YMCA meant possibly putting oneself in harm's way. As a result, only a small percentage of students at Thompson (a few student athletes) took part in exercise of any kind outside of gym class once a week. Many kids weren't even allowed to stay after school to attend basketball practice because by the time practice was over, it would be getting dark out . . . which meant it wouldn't be safe for them to walk home at that time of night. And it should be noted, aside from the risk of getting caught in the crossfire of a stray bullet, anyone walking on the street also ran the risk of getting mugged or recruited by local gang members.

I quickly learned that if I had something important to give to a student (such as a bag of groceries or even a toy), I was better off taking it directly to their house. Sending a child home with anything valuable meant putting them at risk of having them approached on their way home by someone who'd seek to steal the item, and often also beat them up in the process. Even a benign item like a toy, which would seem at first glance to be useless to a teenager or grown adult, would often be forcefully taken, as that item could be sold to someone else.

It was also commonplace for young boys to become recruited by street gangs at an early age. Gangs have been in Chicago since the 1880s and in recent decades have spent considerable time honing their recruiting skills. Preying on young children who are searching for an identity, knowing there's often no loving family to protect them and keep them safe, gang members know exactly how to convert a young boy into the newest member of their gang. Commonly, they'll entice youths with desirable items, such as video games or Air Jordan athletic shoes. Knowing the boy's parents likely couldn't afford $200 shoes, gang leaders are making these kids an offer that's hard for them to refuse.

Once they bring their new recruits into the fold, the gang will, at first, spend time lavishing them with attention and gifts, in order for them to be seen as "comrades" to be trusted. Once a level of trust is clearly established, the boy would be asked to run "errands" for the gang—essentially working as a drug runner. Getting caught carrying a large amount of drugs would mean instant prison time for adults and for teens over a certain age, but for a boy as young as seven years old, there would be no legal repercussion. I learned from many students' personal accounts this tactic was how a lot of the boys I worked with initially got recruited into the South Side gang life.

Frustrated at seeing so many students having fallen into the gang lifestyle through this need for belonging and love, I searched for a way to break the cycle. I knew the work I was doing—particularly providing counseling to my students—was impactful, but it was clear some kids, especially the older boys, had a hard time relating to me in the same way they could relate to someone who had grown up in a similar environment. I felt fortunate to run across the In My Shoes program, which at the time was being organized by the Schwab Rehabilitation Center. In My Shoes is a violence prevention program that brings former gang members, who now have disabilities as a result of their gang involvement, into schools to speak about their experiences. Almost all of the program's speakers are in wheelchairs as a result of their injuries, and most are paraplegic or quadriplegic from being shot.

The In My Shoes program cost a few hundred dollars per talk, but I knew it would be a valuable presentation, so I convinced my principals at both schools to use grant funding to pay for the presentations. I was glad to see the speakers were even more impressive than I'd anticipated. Two men and one woman told their stories to my students about how they were once in the students' shoes, sitting in a lecture hall, hating school and wanting nothing but for the school day to end so they could get back to their friends in the gang. But one day, each of the speakers' lives changed forever when they were shot—usually as a result of a drug deal gone bad or because of an encounter with a rival gang. In almost all of the cases, the intended target was someone else in the room, not them. They recounted the details of the day it happened and the consequences, while my students sat listening in rapt attention.

The speakers from In My Shoes bluntly described how their lives had been flipped upside down after being shot. They told the students how challenging it was to learn to live life all over again, in a wheelchair, and how they had to make it a habit to adjust their body every few hours so they didn't get bed sores, which can—as it became more popularly known from the case of Christopher

Reeves—be deadly if they become infected. They also spoke about dealing with the crippling depression and anxiety they experienced and about the challenges of losing not just the use of their limbs, but their entire identity and support system (which previously had been comprised of fellow gang members).

These humbled men and women passed around a colostomy bag like the type they had to wear, and explained to the students how debilitating it was to not have control of such a basic bodily function as going to the bathroom. They spoke about going through months and months of painful physical rehabilitation at the hospital, only to be released and find that life at home was, for many, worse than being at the hospital. Their homes were not equipped for living in a wheelchair, which meant that if there was even an inch-high step leading into their house, they were stuck and could not get inside without someone around to lift up their wheelchair for them. Showering, making food, and getting into bed took these people extreme amounts of effort and practice in order to be able to do each task on their own without having someone to help them. Not being able to afford a home health care worker, they were often left on their own to deal with every aspect of their lives.

Interestingly enough, many of the stories involved situations my students could relate to—joining a gang at an early age, not growing up in a two-parent family—but I could not relate to. However, one woman's story stuck out to me in a way I will never forget. Unlike the other speakers, Melanie was not in a wheelchair. She told the story about how a few years earlier, she'd been working as a real estate agent. When the recession hit and the real estate market was severely affected, it became harder and harder for her to provide for her family. Melanie was married with a young son, and the family relied heavily on her income to get by. A friend of hers sold marijuana, and he offered her the chance to make some money, if she would (as he said) "just help me out."

The plan he described was simple: he would drive her to an apartment, hand her the drugs, she would go in to the buyer's place and make the exchange. Eventually becoming financially desperate enough, Melanie convinced herself to participate in his admittedly illegal scheme.

After a few months, she was able to generate enough money making drug-for-cash exchanges that she started to spend more of her time working with the dealer and less time trying to get real estate jobs. One day, she was in the middle of what she thought was a "routine transaction" when someone pulled out a gun and shot her. Melanie's story impacted me greatly, because as I listened to her sharing how she'd gotten involved in this illegal and dangerous enterprise, it seemed like something that could easily happen to me, or to anyone. She had a college degree and never intended to get deep into the drug business, but she was doing something she thought was a temporary fix in order to help her family survive.

Each speaker talked about how hard it was to leave the gang lifestyle behind after they'd returned home from the hospital. In fact, one of them actually returned to the gang life afterward—*even though he was now living out of a wheelchair as a paraplegic*. He said the gang life was so ingrained in who he was that he had no idea how to live life in any other way. Sadly, it wasn't until he was shot a second time—and had to go back to the rehabilitation center to recover from this second life-threatening injury—that he was able to leave the gang life behind.

They concluded their talk by emphasizing how important it was for students not to join a gang in the first place. "Because once you're in," Melanie declared, "it is *so* challenging, and often dangerous, to leave."

While this was prudent advice, I knew many of the students in the audience were already deeply involved in one gang or another. I raised my hand to ask a question of the speakers: "What advice would you have for a student who is already in a gang, but wants to get out?"

Melanie responded with this chilling admonition: "The only way for a student in that situation to truly get out is to move out of the neighborhood and attend a different school. Without completely removing yourself from the environment, you've got *no* chance of leaving the gang life alive."

It seemed as though wherever I turned, I was confronted with more examples of why there was a need for an urban boarding school. I often felt I was less a therapist and more a parent to many of my students, as I often bought food to give to those kids with whom I worked who came to school starving after not having had anything to eat since the school lunch the day before. I also bought socks, shoes, clothes and underwear for students on a regular basis. When I got wind of the fact that Marilyn, one of my students, slept in her school uniform because she didn't have any pajamas, I bought her some and watched her tear up in joy at owning her first pair of pajamas. I held many more than one crying student in my arms the day after their best friend was shot and killed or after their parent was taken to jail. Indeed, there are some terrific parents out there whose children go to CPS and who are doing the best job they can while being dealt a tough set of cards. However, I also encountered countless parents over the years whose behavior demonstrated they were not "fit" to be parents. The second time I encountered a suicidal child and had to call her parent, I remember being very sensitive, even gentle, as I relayed the news to the student's mother. I made sure to sound as reassuring as possible, saying, "Don't worry, your daughter is doing fine, but I wanted to let you know that earlier today, she expressed suicidal ideation."

I was shocked when her mother callously replied, "Do you think I care? Deal with it!" and hung up the phone on me.

It became very clear a lot of the social/emotional issues (students who were depressed, suicidal, etc. and those who were acting out behaviorally) were directly related to what was happening in their home environments. There are hundreds of studies indicating the importance of a child's establishing a healthy attachment to their caregivers. Additionally, current research has shown that the brains of children who grow up in homes where they aren't demonstrably loved and don't feel safe can become wired to engage in more unhealthy, risk-taking behaviors throughout childhood, as well as into adulthood.

In his 2016 book *Helping Children Succeed*, Paul Tough makes several salient points that touch the heart of what I experienced working with students at CPS:

- As of 2013, the majority of United States public school students fell below the threshold considered low income" by the government. As a result, the many obstacles that often come with teaching low income students must become a national priority.

- Unstable environments can create biological changes in the growing brains and bodies of young children which makes it more challenging for them later in life to learn how to process information and properly regulate their emotions.

- Environmental factors such as poor nutrition, neglect, and exposure to violence can lead to chronic levels of stress in children that impede their physiological and psychological development.

- Environmental stress can also impact brain development in the prefrontal cortex, which controls intellectual functions that allow a child to regulate their emotions. Ongoing stress in a child's environment can make it challenging for them to respond to setbacks and can lead to fighting and other acting-out behavior.

- Ongoing environmental stress can also lead to impaired academic performance due to the impact on the prefrontal cortex.

- 2016 research from the National Center for Biotechnology Information shows us that the development of certain non-cognitive skills such as self-control, perseverance, optimism, and conscientiousness are skills that improve outcomes for low-income students.

- A Kaiser Foundation Hospitals study of 17,000 individuals found that patients with more than four adverse childhood experiences (ACE's) were twice as likely to be diagnosed with cancer, twice as likely to be diagnosed with heart disease, twice as likely to have liver disease, and four times as likely to be diagnosed with emphysema as adults. Higher ACE scores were also tied to higher risks of depression, anxiety, and suicide as adults. They were also found to be twice as likely to smoke and seven times more likely to become alcoholics in adulthood.

Taken as a whole, these research findings point to the importance of how much environmental factors influence a child's ability to function—both on a social/emotional level, and also academically—in an academic setting and how low-income students who are exposed to stress are often doubly disadvantaged from an early age, a factor that compounds the achievement gap over time.

TEN

• • •

The holidays were upon us, which to me has always been my favorite time of year. As a kid, I loved Thanksgiving, which meant eating copious amounts of delicious food and time spent having fun and laughing with extended family. Thanksgiving meant love and cozy feelings of warmth and safety. After Thanksgiving had passed by, I'd always spend the next month of the year excitedly anticipating Christmas.

Growing up, I recall my family wasn't wealthy, as both of my parents worked in education. However, I always had what seemed like an abundance of presents under the Christmas tree. We would typically eat delicious, home-cooked food, bake Christmas cookies, listen to Christmas songs, and drive around looking at the extravagant Christmas lights. There were many wealthy subdivisions in my hometown, with multi-million dollar homes that were decked out, "Clark Griswold-style."

Many of these homes spent tens of thousands of dollars on lights and decorations each year, and it was quite a sight to behold.

One of my other favorite Christmas traditions also involved taking a day trip into Chicago, where we would walk up and down Michigan Avenue, buying hot chocolate and warm, roasted chestnuts along the way. We'd eat dinner by the "big tree" in the Walnut Room at Macy's, walk around Christkindlmarket (the German market), and then go ice skating.

In contrast, for many of the CPS students living in poverty, I swiftly found out the holidays were the worst time of year. Not only did many kids go without a delicious Thanksgiving feast or Christmas presents, but being home for two weeks in a row was hell for those who lacked heat or access to regular meals. It was even worse for students who were the victims of abuse, to be locked up in the same house as their abuser for two solid weeks, without being able to escape to school as a safe haven.

When I heard about the "Letters to Santa program" being sponsored by the *Chicago Sun-Times*, I knew I had to get involved. I applied and was accepted into the program, which involved the *Sun-Times* finding donors who would buy gifts for students based on their "letters to Santa" requests.

A month later, the presents started to roll in. It was an incredible amount of work trying to organize hundreds of Christmas presents, which involved my putting in even more hours after school and on weekends. But by the time the day came to hand out the presents, all of the time and energy was worth it. My husband dressed up in a borrowed Santa suit (four sizes too large for him), and we went from room to room giving gifts to the students. Many of them were so excited to get presents they shrieked out loud and hugged "Santa" in gratitude. A lot of the younger students' parents had come to watch the festivities, and many teared up watching their children being so happy.

While many educators spend the two weeks of winter vacation relaxing, I spent every minute of my time preparing for the next semester ahead. I found a specialty bookstore on the north side of Chicago and spent hundreds of dollars there for books on cognitive behavioral therapy for children, play therapy and art therapy, plus more therapeutic games I could use with my students. The first semester had been wildly challenging, and more often than I would have liked to admit, I had felt ill-equipped to handle situations that were thrown at me.

By that time, I'd realized being a teacher in a CPS school was an incredibly challenging job and I was constantly in awe of how hard the teachers worked in my schools, often for little thanks. But one benefit teachers had was being surrounded by dozens of peers who were there for support and advice at any given time. As the only social worker at both of my schools, I did not get to enjoy that benefit.

I loved that I was able to work independently, but when I was faced with a situation I was unsure about or unprepared for, it was often extremely challenging. The work was routinely isolating and emotionally draining.

Spending hours of each day around students who were dealing with very serious issues, such as witnessing homicides, being kicked out of their homes in the middle of the night, or going without food, meant that on a visceral level I took on a great deal of these stressors myself. Constantly being called upon to address this amount of psychological and emotional stress eventually began to weigh me down.

I was known at both of my schools for being energetic, positive and perky, and those things were true. These aspects were a part of who I was, certainly, but they were also traits I knew I had to present with each day because my students deserved that from me. If I was having a bad day, there was no way I could bring any of that to school with me. My students were going through so much trauma in their lives, I owed them 100% of myself. That meant not just my undivided attention, love and respect, but I owed them a smile, and for me to be a light in their lives when they otherwise may not have anything else to light their way.

After being energetically "on" at all times during the day, the minute I got into my car to go home each evening, I could feel myself practically collapsing with the pressure weighing on me. When I'd get home, I had zero energy left, much to the dismay of my husband, who wanted me to come home, cook dinner and engage in witty banter. Because I was exposed to such negativity on a regular basis, I stopped watching and reading the news. I soon stopped watching anything that wasn't comedic, as I felt so overexposed to such real, raw aspects of life that the last thing I wanted to do was watch a TV show about a rape or murder. I knew those things were all too real for many of the students I worked with, and I needed TV to be a mindless, albeit temporary, escape from reality.

Similarly, working so closely with trauma and despair on a regular basis impacted my entire worldview in various ways. After spending the majority of my waking hours working with children and teens who were angry, anxious, grieving and/or suicidal, I realized childhood was not always the carefree time it had been for me. Aside from the issues my students dealt with that were specific to living in poverty, I also saw other societal factors I'm sure had huge implications on their growth and development, regardless of what socioeconomic bracket they grew up in.

During my upbringing in the 80s, I grew up without cable television and was sheltered from seeing PG-13 or R movies until I was practically an adult. In contrast, most all of the kids I worked with were playing violent video games—many of which were so graphic I would have had to cover my eyes—and so accustomed to seeing sex and violence on TV and in movies that they were not shocked by either. It was not uncommon for kids as young as preschool to play these video games and to watch R-rated movies, with or without adult supervision. Unfortunately, early exposure to violence in the media can lead to students exhibiting more aggressive behavior with their peers and engaging in sexual activity at younger ages (American Psychological Association, 2013).

And then... there was the internet. Being born in 1983, I technically fall into the camp of being a "Millennial", but I object to this categorization for one main reason: the average Millennial grew up having cell phones and the internet, and I did not. Rather, I and those who were my cohorts grew up in a unique, in-between time, such that we knew both the pre- and post-internet worlds.

We didn't get the internet in my house until I was just starting high school, and I got my first "car phone" when I was 16. It was to be kept in my car, as texting hadn't been invented yet. I don't recall being introduced to Google until the end of college. As a result, I didn't grow up in an era where information was so readily at my fingertips, as it is for today's youth. And I also didn't have to worry about cyberbullying—a term that wasn't even coined at the time.

Cyberbullying essentially refers to any type of bullying behavior that occurs through the use of any form of technology. That could mean anything from email to Facebook to texting to tweeting. The most common form of cyberbullying is relational—insulting, threatening, harassing, and intimating—and numerous studies have found conclusive evidence to link the skyrocketing rate of relational cyberbullying to depression and even self-harm and suicide.

The phenomenon known as cyberbullying has become an epidemic in middle schools, high schools, and even elementary schools across the country, and my CPS students were not immune to this. Because cyberbullying adds a layer of anonymity to predatory attacking students, it allows kids who would normally not have the courage to belittle someone to their face to "speak" hateful, injurious words toward another student. Pre-internet bullying could not be done from the comfort of one's home, but with the onset of cyberbullying, the school's role as temporary guardian has been required to adapt, and various legal issues have arisen, as well.

If an instance of cyberbullying has happened when students were at home, teachers and principals have struggled with what to do about it at school. However, they were certainly responsible for doing their part to provide solutions and support, as its effects necessarily will have carried over into the classroom. In my experience, it was common for students to run into my office crying at the beginning of the school day because they had been bullied the night before, and they couldn't bear to have to sit next to the offending bully all day in class.

In a few cases of cyberbullying, if the school had not intervened, it could have proven deadly. In these scenarios, a group of girls were found to be ganging up on another girl and—via technology—telling her she was ugly and should die. They persisted in taunting her and urged her to kill herself. Fortunately, news of this harassment was leaked to school officials who quickly got involved and were able to intervene before it was too late.

In another example, a group of girls pretended to be a boy, and they made up fake emails to send to another girl in their class. Similar to the "infamous" Manti Te'o case (in which a romantic hoax was set up by a cyberbully), this girl was "catfished" into thinking she was in a relationship with a boy. The group eventually told her it was all a prank, but the girl was so ashamed, she became suicidal as a result.

It's not only difficult to ask a student who has become the victim of such bullying to "attend class anyhow" and "do their best" to learn when they are under such emotional duress, but these emotional traumas often carry into adulthood, as well. One of my most vivid childhood memories stems from a similar occurrence. I was at a slumber party and someone decided to play a game called, "If we were on a desert island, who would you kill first?" The girls in the group unanimously decided to kill me, using the excuse: "You're so quiet." Over twenty years later, I still remember the pain I felt in that moment.

I knew cyberbullying was not something I could stop for good, but I wanted to put out my best efforts. I found a detective who worked for the Chicago Police Department (CPD) whose main job was handling cyberbullying offenses. I brought him into both of my schools to have him give one talk to students and another to parents. During his talk with the students, the detective explained that cyberbullying is something the CPD takes very seriously. He told them if he found out about any incidents of cyberbullying happening at the school, he would go to the home to investigate, and students could even be arrested.

This certainly seemed to unnerve many of the students in the audience who had previously only seem the repercussions of cyberbullying as a meeting with the principal, where they'd be sternly asked not to do it again. When the detective spoke to parents, he explained this same legal procedure to parents, but also talked about how if anything were to happen as a result of their child being a cyberbully—i.e., if the victim were to kill themselves as a result—the parent could also be held legally responsible. He also provided the parents with valuable information about ways they could keep tabs on their child's online behavior.

Most of the parents in the room said their child had a cell phone, but didn't "allow" their parent to know the password, a practice the detective said needed to stop immediately. He explained how, in this day and age, it was the parent's responsibility to not only know their child's password, but to check their phone regularly, as well as their social media accounts. He also gave them an in-depth lesson on the things kids often do in order to try to fool their parents into not really knowing what they're doing. For example, we learned kids often use code to talk to friends, and many students set up a fake Facebook account their parents know about, while also having a separate account where they post inappropriate pictures and messages their parents would not want them to discover.

In short, I saw firsthand how challenging it is to be a kid these days. After witnessing so many of the challenges and obstacles that exist for young people today, which weren't around when I was growing up, my work life started to seep into my personal life, and I started to shift my perspective on becoming a parent. My husband and I had always talked about having children ("sometime during the next few years"), but working around kids going through so much trauma made me question this. I saw so many incredibly unhappy kids and wasn't sure I wanted to be the force that would purposefully bring a child into a world that could be so cruel.

Interestingly enough, I'd generally thought of myself as an optimist . . . but when it came to having kids, I felt pessimistic about the decision to have kids. Still, I regularly felt drawn to the idea of adoption—in fact, there were many students I worked with whom I would have instantly adopted if the opportunity presented itself. It was clear to me, so many of these students would have been able to become successful in life if they just had a safe, loving home environment to mitigate the challenges they were confronted with on a regular basis.

But my husband was immersed in a different world through his job, and he thought my shift in perspective was ludicrous. This difference in how we saw things became one of the many rifts in our marriage that grew wider and wider the longer I worked in CPS.

My students also faced additional pressures that didn't seem to pose an issue when I was growing up, relating to academic expectations. Thankfully, I was a good student, and succeeding and advancing in school wasn't an issue for me. I worked hard to get good grades but was never especially stressed out by school . . . and getting at least one college degree was never a question. In contrast, the community where my students lived was the polar opposite. Dropping out of school was normal, and, as of 2016, only 57% of African American males in Chicago Public Schools graduate high school. According to the University of Chicago Consortium on School Research, a 2014 study indicates only 14% of CPS 9th graders graduate college by their 25th birthday.

As such, the students I worked with seemed to fall into two camps: those motivated to succeed academically and those who had given up. The kids who fell into the latter category often expressed concerns about even living to be 18, which was reasonable, when so many had seen their peers, older family members and neighbors lose their lives at a young age due to gun violence. For these students, it made sense to spend their time at school goofing off and having fun, rather than learning subjects they had no interest in. Heck, they weren't sure they would live to see their 16th birthday! And they most certainly didn't feel a need to master any subject matter in order to get into college. Joining a gang and getting involved with drugs and other high risk behaviors was a welcome distraction for many whose lives, as they described it to me, "hardly seemed worth living." Many students told me they felt they were just killing time until they ended up dead or in jail.

Still, there were also a select number of students who did have academic ambitions and for them, life posed a different set of challenges. I acknowledge there are a handful of excellent public schools in Chicago, but they are few and far between. Most CPS schools are not providing the high caliber of academic instruction that all students deserve. This being so, the Southside students who *are* academically motivated have a hard time receiving the quality education they need to be able to compete. As Paul Tough wrote in *Helping Children Succeed*: "Researchers found that even for students who do not ever get suspended, being in a classroom where a high number of students get suspended was correlated with a drop in test scores. Being in a classroom where your peers are more likely to be suspended, even if you never got in trouble yourself, created an atmosphere that was less conducive to your academic success" (2016).

I saw, firsthand, how both the school and home atmosphere affected the students, particularly at Thompson. Jonathan had a much higher number of students who were motivated to succeed academically . . . but at Thompson, such students were few and far between. It should be pointed out that being motivated to learn meant very little in a classroom where it was nearly impossible to get anything done—due to the seemingly constant stream of fights or disruptions—and where teacher burn-out seemed to be regularly at play, as well.

When it came time to take the ISAT (Illinois Standardized Assessment Test), more than one student reported having panic attacks (not even during the test itself, but *prior* to the test), because they felt so unprepared and were worried about their academic future. I started going into the classrooms to teach students about meditation and positive visualization techniques they could use to prepare and to help them stay more calm and focused during the exam. But the reality was that even the "good students" at the schools where I worked had little chance of getting into a respected high school.

The disparity between the South Side and West Side schools in Chicago (both of which are primarily minority populations) and the North Side schools (which are primarily white populations) was vast. Though Chicago Public Schools often gets a bad rap, I want to make explicitly clear that there are many great schools in CPS, and there are thousands of exceptional teachers located in schools on the South, West, and North sides of the city. However, it is a widely held assumption that north side schools are often of a higher caliber which often stems from being better resourced. Because these schools are located in wealthier neighborhoods, PTA fundraising efforts could bring in over a million dollars per year, per school which can be used for additional resources—anything from providing iPads for all of the students, to taking students on college field trips, to hiring additional staff members. It was upsetting to me there weren't better options for South Side students. Even for students who had sufficiently high test scores to qualify for a selective enrollment magnet school on the North Side of Chicago (where the vast majority of higher performing schools are concentrated), chances were slim that transportation could be worked out to get them there.

For many students on the South Side of Chicago, getting to one of the North Side schools would require walking to the bus, taking the bus to a train, transferring to another train, transferring to another bus, and walking to the school. This process was not only cumbersome and time-consuming—it could take over two hours in each direction—but it was also often unsafe. On Chicago's South Side, it's not a good idea for young teens to be leaving their house so early that it's dark out and to come home when it's dark again at the end of the day.

As a result, many students and their families did not feel comfortable having them attend a school outside of their neighborhood. That meant countless bright students, full of potential, ended up attending a subpar neighborhood school, often full of students whose grades wouldn't have gotten them in anywhere else. At these schools, having fewer academic success stories and more behavioral issues than most selective enrollment schools, talented kids who were *not* bullies were likely to be bullied and picked on, intimidated into joining a gang, or drop out of school—due to social struggles, academic struggles or both.

ELEVEN

• • •

After spending the summer reading everything I thought would help me better serve my students, I was excited to get back to school. And I was thrilled when I was assigned my own office! The school was not nearly filled to capacity—due to families leaving the violent neighborhood in droves—and there were a number of empty classrooms being unused. I hunted around thrift shops until I found an old, dilapidated loveseat. True, it was in terrible shape, but it was colorful, which I loved, and had character. I knew how important it was for my students to feel comfortable in my office (or anywhere in the school), and I tried to make my new office as cozy and welcoming as I could. I set up the loveseat, a colorful rug, a papasan chair, and bean bag chairs I'd purchased for the occasion, to make a special area for groups.

Unlike my space at Jonathan, I had enough room at Thompson in this office for my desk, the comfortable group seating area, and a long table, and it still had tons of ample room. This was the perfect setup for me to do a lot of the group activities, which I had always wanted to do with my students, but wasn't able to because of space constraints.

At the end of all of my individual and group sessions with students, I began ending the session with a request for each student to take a strip of construction paper and write down either something they liked about themselves, something they were proud of, or something that made them happy. Counseling sessions were often emotionally tough, as students were talking about situations ranging from being homeless to feeling alone to being abused, and I wanted to make sure we ended on a positive note before I sent them back to their classroom. So I'd then take these pieces of construction paper and loop each one around another one, making a long chain, and as I attached more and more loops, the chains began stretching all around the walls of my office, like colorful paper holiday lights. This inspiring, vibrant addition enhanced the room's atmosphere and seemed to catch the eye of many of my incoming students.

During my first year, I had taught a Pilates class to a few students before school once a week. I wasn't a certified Pilates instructor, but had taken classes for years, and since I felt horrified at how little most of my students exercised, I wanted to teach them a form of exercise that was both fun and could also be done at home. This gave me the idea: with my newly minted office space, what if I offered to teach yoga to my students? I wasn't a certified yoga instructor, but I knew the basics and felt it would be a good way to engage the students in an all-around positive practice that would get them moving while also building their mind-body connection.

One drawback was the linoleum floor in my office: it meant the students would need mats. I didn't have any extra money to spend on items like yoga mats, so I resorted to being resourceful.

One day I spent an afternoon calling all—and I mean *all*—of the yoga studios in Chicago. I asked each of the studio owners if they had any spare, unclaimed old mats that had been left at their studio that were worthy of donation. Fortunately, many of them said they did, and I was free to have them if I could find a way to pick them up. I spent the following weekend driving around to pick up these yoga mats and then dropping them off at my office, so I could go back out and pick up another load. All in all, I collected over 50 yoga mats! I could only use about 10 at once at Thompson, but I knew the gym teacher at Jonathan would be happy to use them in his classes, as well. I also felt hopeful that one day I would have more space at Jonathan to be able to do yoga with my students there on a regular basis.

I started teaching meditation, guided visualization and yoga to as many of my students as I could. Students who were previously unable to manage their emotions, even with the help of prescribed psychotropic medications, started to beg me to let them take part in a guided visualization exercise at the end of their sessions. They would lie on a yoga mat with the lights out and with my special IKEA light plugged in for soft lighting. I'd also have some quiet Zen music playing in the background. I would then walk them through a simple visualization exercise to help them find "their happy place" and then would lead them through a series of breathing exercises.

It delighted me to witness students who I've never seen calm before, all of a sudden become centered. Many of them told me the times they spent doing this exercise in my classroom were the only times in their lives when they truly felt calm or experienced quietness. I knew it was common for my students to live in homes with anywhere from 1-12 siblings, and therefore nearly impossible for them to ever find a moment alone.

Teaching yoga was a bit trickier, as kids typically aren't able to flow through a series of yoga poses in the same way adults generally can. Instead, it often required numerous requests from me to stay on their mat and not to tease the student next to them, as well as reminders that yoga is supposed to be a "silent activity." Indeed, it was commonplace for my students to either fall out of a warrior pose in a state of silly laughter or for them to complain, "This is too hard on my muscles!"

These students were only used to getting about an hour of gym time per month, and at first, yoga was practically an extreme sport for many of them. Though virtually everyone started off skeptically— especially my groups for older boys—it didn't take long for them to learn it and love it. Word started to get around the school quickly, and soon, I was approached multiple times a day from other students who'd heard about the fun "yoga class that makes you calm" and wanted to join in. I ended up ordering multiple books, posters and other resources to help me teach these skills to students of all ages, including a poster that labeled each yoga pose by an animal name, in order to appeal to younger children.

Shortly after, I found myself attending a conference during which I took a workshop called Calm Classroom. The seminar introduced us to a series of brief exercises—revolving around deep breathing and meditation practices—that can typically be implemented in less than five minutes. I loved the workshop and bought their book to take back with me to my schools. I met with both of my principals and excitedly shared the research I had found that shows how impactful it can be to do breathing exercises on a school-wide level. I proposed an idea where we could carve out five minutes during the morning announcements, during which the person reading the announcements over the intercom could lead the whole school in one of the Calm Classroom exercises. To my dismay, both of the principals balked at this idea.

One of my favorite Zen proverbs says, "Those who don't have time to meditate for twenty minutes, should meditate for two days." Similarly, I knew if my schools could spare me a measly five minutes each morning for these exercises, teachers would soon yield a far greater return later in the day, as their students would likely be more focused, calmer, more productive and kinder to one another. It took a great deal of convincing, but after a few months I finally persuaded the administration to try it on a school-wide basis.

This was a step in the right direction, but unfortunately it didn't stick. The principals may have requested all teachers to participate, but I would often walk by a classroom during this "Calm Classroom time" and I'd notice they were allowing their kids to talk to each other and play around the room without even making an attempt to spend the five minutes on the breathing exercises being offered.

While I couldn't mandate what teachers did with their students in their classrooms, I *did* have the ability to influence students in other ways. Seeing I'd made some inroads with the "Calm

Classroom" morning exercises (which, to Jonathan's credit, they eventually did start to implement with fidelity at a later point), I began seeking out more opportunities to bring programming to the entire school at a time.

When I was in high school, whenever we were called to the auditorium to hear a motivational speaker, the rest of my classmates would groan and complain, but I secretly loved it. As an adult, I knew those same speakers would often explore topics that might not sink in with my students immediately, but would plant seeds in their minds that could sprout up later in life, when the time was right for them to fully assimilate the information.

I began bringing in speakers who covered a wide variety of topics, ranging from the usual anti-violence and anti-drug initiatives to sex education to motivational themes and more. One of my favorite speakers was Lloyd Bachrach, who was born with a congenital bone deficiency that left his legs unusually small. He competed in the International Paralympic Games, despite doctors telling his parents that he would never have a normal life. Lloyd spoke about the lessons he's learned going through life faced with challenges that many would deem to be insurmountable, and I was so inspired by his story that I later interviewed him on my podcast, and we have stayed in contact to this day. It was incredible seeing so many of my students—who had faced tremendous adversity in their lives, often to the point of being suicidal—tell me that they were moved to tears by Lloyd's story. One of my students who had been chronically suicidal for years told me that hearing Lloyd speak was going to be a reminder to her going forward that she really *could* overcome the challenges in her life.

TWELVE

• • •

also loved taking students on inspiring, eye-opening field trips, but field trips carried with them multiple extra challenges. I first had to get permission from my principal, and then they had to get permission from the area office... which could take weeks or even months. Then, I had to get permission from each student's parent—which was a much bigger ordeal than it should have been— and as a result, a lot of kids weren't able to go on great field trips, since their parent wasn't available to sign a permission slip.

The biggest hurdle, though, was the funding for transportation. Because one school bus cost nearly $500 a day to use—and to take a full grade level of 40-60 students meant at least two school buses—I was very limited, in terms of what I was able to do for the students. There were a few organizations, like Chicago's truly amazing Museum of Contemporary Art, which graciously funded the cost of school bus transportation. For other events, I had to fundraise on my own or appeal to the school's principal to try to help me find funding.

One organization that (to my excitement) provided buses was the S.M.A.R.T. program conducted by the Cook County Sheriff's Office. This program focused on educating eighth-grade students about the criminal justice system. First, an officer from the jail would come to speak to my students about what offenses most commonly landed teenagers in jail, and then the following week we would all take a field trip to go visit and tour the jail. During the first component, the officers candidly answered questions from the students about how the criminal justice system worked, and many students were shocked to hear their answers.

For example, Officer Parker, one of the female officers, explained to the girls (the classes were divided by gender for this program) that a large portion of women in the jail were there because of crimes their boyfriends had committed, which *they* ended up getting roped into. Many students, both boys and girls, were also shocked to realize that if they were in the car with someone who, for example, was in possession of cocaine, every person in the car could be arrested for possession of cocaine, no matter who it belonged to. Similarly, if a student is at a party where police discover drugs, that student could be held liable, even if they didn't know about the drugs.

The next week, we boarded our school buses to head to the Cook County Jail. On the way there, the girls had been loudly singing in unison to Rhianna songs, and laughing and having fun. As soon as the bus parked and Officer Parker got on the bus, she told them to immediately stop what they were doing and pay attention. Many of the girls stopped, but some continued with their sidebar conversations, which caused Officer Parker to yell, "Everybody listen… NOW!" Silence fell over the bus.

Our Cook County Jail tour guide became very stern and explained they needed to take everything she said very seriously going forward. "If anyone does *not* heed the rules you are being asked to follow, regarding not bringing paraphernalia into the jail—and we will cover what that entails" (even items such as cell phones, Chapstick and gum were forbidden)—"those items will be confiscated and you could face criminal prosecution."

71

We—both the students and all school staff members—were also told we'd need to temporarily turn over to them any jewelry aside from tiny stud earrings. Anything larger, they explained, could conceivably be used as a weapon.

After getting off of the bus, we were instructed to stand in a single file line, as we waited in the cold to enter the jail. Once inside, each girl had to walk through the metal detectors. If anyone made even a peep of a noise, they were immediately reprimanded by the other officers who had joined Officer Parker. They escorted us through the jail and the girls started to realize the severity of the situation. As we walked by one jail cell after another, the locked up women cat-called to the girls and shouted lewd comments to some of them, yelling taunts about how they wanted the girls to get locked up so they could be lovers. I saw looks of terror appear on the faces of many of my students.

When we got to one of the larger rooms, the students were able to go into an empty cell to take a closer look at it. I joined the girls and was shocked at how minuscule and incredibly bare-boned the cell was. The toilet was in the middle of the cell, which meant there was absolutely no privacy, since each imprisoned woman had a cellmate. The mattress was flimsy and hard, and there was nothing else in the room besides a clouded mirror and a sink. The girls gasped at the gravity of the situation and exclaimed how they could *never* live like that. We also took a tour of the communal shower area and were shown the two items the women are given when they enter jail: a tiny bar of soap and a miniature toothbrush.

After each girl had the chance to walk into a cell (it was so small, only a few had room to be in a cell at once), they were asked to sit on the benches in the middle of the room. The officers then asked two of the women who had been locked up in a cell to join us in the center of the room. After the guards unlocked the cells of these women, they came to stand right in front of me and my students. The girls were visibly shaken up at the thought of these women in orange jumpsuits standing within inches of them. And though I knew we would never put their safety in jeopardy, I could understand their concern.

I'd never gone through a "scared straight" program when I was their age, but if I had, I would have been equally terrified. The women spoke honestly about what it was like living in the jail, and they also imparted the wisdom they had learned over the years, such as, "I wish I would have listened to my counselor and studied harder in school" and "I wish I would have never gotten into the car with my boyfriend."

They spoke about how challenging it was to be imprisoned and passed around an example of the meal—a bologna sandwich on dry bread—they'd receive for breakfast, lunch and dinner.

Of particular interest, too, was hearing about how, after they'd been put in jail, the majority of their family members and friends stopped visiting them and stopped calling them altogether. Many of them were in jail because of gang ties, and they spoke about how no one from the gang maintained contact after their incarceration.

Our last stop entailed visiting the jail "school," which was a single room with a few desks. My students got to meet some of the "students" attending classes, who proceeded to tell my girls how going to school was the best part of their day. They adamantly urged my students to continue getting a good education and to avoid ending up in jail, as they had.

Even as an adult who'd never committed a crime in my life, going to jail was an eerie experience I'll never forget. It's impossible to tour a jail and not leave thinking, "Wow, I thought I'd previously been someone who abided by the law, but now I'm *really* never going to commit a crime."

Once we returned to school, I had my students fill out an evaluation of the field trip. The general consensus seemed to be it was a valuable, soul-stirring experience and gave them a lot to think about. I'll never know if that jail trip saved any of my students from ending up in jail, but I like to think it did.

THIRTEEN

· · ·

When I thought about how to provide additional programming to my students, it wasn't just about how to deter them from making negative choices—I also knew it was equally important to inspire them to make positive changes in their lives. Ever since I'd first stepped foot into a CPS cafeteria, I had been appalled at the low-quality school lunches being offered. One day, I even took a picture of one of the trays of food my students were eating from, because literally every single item was some shade of brown, or beige: a brown colored piece of indistinguishable meat, a beige roll, brown vegetables (I think they may have been very old, overly cooked sweet potatoes that had been rolled in sugar)... and, of course, supplemented with chocolate milk.

Within my own life, I had, in recent years, undergone a personal health transformation during which I'd realized how important good nutrition and exercise is, not just for my body, but also for my mental health. I'd come to see just how much better I felt physically and emotionally when I would eat a clean, vegetable-centric diet, and when I ate minimal amounts of sugar, dairy, wheat, and junk food. I could think more clearly and would have more focus, exponentially more energy, and generally greater happiness.

Looking back, I couldn't believe I'd wasted so many years of my life not treating my body with the respect it deserves. I knew that, while the quality of their diet wasn't the sole factor making life challenging for my students, I knew if they could improve their diet and prioritize at least some amount of regular exercise, it could make a dramatic difference. Research points out that good nutrition is critical for a child's cognitive development, and I knew a healthier diet could lead to a greater number of students being happier, having more energy, and who may even experience fewer symptoms of ADHD and oppositional defiance disorder.

I did some research and found a program that offered schools grant money to build a salad bar in their school. A salad bar!! Overjoyed at the idea of providing students with healthy options, I knew establishing habits of good nutrition in childhood and the teen years could have a significant impact on their health for decades to come.

After starting the grant applications for both of my schools, I noticed I'd have to get clearance from both principals first. I excitedly told them about the opportunity but was disappointed to find out neither principal thought their school had the resources to handle a cafeteria salad bar.

Each school only had the bare minimum number of cafeteria workers on hand, and each had a very clear-cut role. There had to be a set number of people working "the line" and serving the students, someone had to take care of taking students' ID information (most of our students qualified for free or reduced lunches, so no one actually paid cash for their lunch except staff members), and another staff member had to be working in the back kitchen. Sadly, neither of my schools had an available staff member on hand to take care of the salad bar. It turned out space was a concern, as well, at both schools.

Though I felt it was unfortunate that I wasn't able to land a free salad bar for my students, I wasn't overly discouraged. I went to my local Whole Foods and filled out an application requesting a gift card for food I could use to teach kids how to cook. And soon I'd started cooking with some of my social work groups, which I found to be a perfect way to teach so many important skill sets to my students: healthy eating practices, math (measuring), how to read a recipe, cooperation, patience, creativity and team building. We focused on making healthy recipes, and I loved introducing them to new foods they had never heard of. I must admit, we also occasionally made some "less healthy" desserts (knowing balance is important).

Overall, these students had the time of their lives, especially when taking a tray of the cookies they'd just made, still warm from the oven, from classroom to classroom, passing out their cookies to the teachers, all of whom were delighted to partake in a homemade treat. More than anything, I loved seeing how my students lit up when they were able to share something they'd created with another human being, who got great joy from that cookie. The benefits of this hands-on "cooking project" were obvious as I watched these students glowing with pride at their accomplishment, many of them appearing more genuinely happy than they had been in months.

The following fall, I ran across a program called Common Threads and discovered—to my delight—that buses were paid for. Sign me up! For three months, the Common Threads program would take fourth-grade students on a weekly after-school trip to a garden in Kenwood Park (just north of where Jonathan was located), where they would learn how to garden *and* cook. Now, while the program itself was free (which eliminated the biggest obstacle), the *next* challenging step entailed finding another chaperone to join me on this weekly excursion.

Most of my colleagues were happy to rush out of school the moment the final bell rang at the end of each school day, so trying to find someone to stay after school for a few hours each week with no extra compensation was an uphill battle. Many North Side schools (and definitely many suburban schools) would have had extra funds to pay teachers for staying after school, but these two South Side schools didn't have this luxury. Apparently, I was the only one who wanted this enough to stay after school with nothing in return but the joy of exposing these kids to new opportunities. I spent a few weeks begging and pleading with every adult in the school, from the counselor to the teachers to even the cafeteria lady. Thankfully, the school nurse agreed to join me for two of the days, and I eventually managed to get other teachers to give one day each.

On our first day at Common Threads, the program staff brought out a variety of foods ranging from vegetables to quinoa and laid them on a table. Upon asking the students if anyone knew what these foods were, what they ended up hearing were many wrong answers. I was completely floored to find quite a few of these students couldn't recognize a tomato, though I shouldn't have been surprised—many of them were only familiar with eating tomatoes in the form of sauce on pizza or ketchup on hamburgers and French fries. Many students also seemed to know potatoes only from eating potato chips.

For many participating students, seeing these bright, colorful veggies in their whole, natural state was an eye-opening experience. Most of them had never helped a parent cook before, and most of them expressed to the Common Threads staff their family only ate "fast food." On special occasions, a few said, their family would go to a restaurant like Ponderosa, but most students had never or rarely had freshly prepared, healthy meals.

Over the course of three months, the students would plant seeds that would grow into everything from vegetables to sunflowers. During the week in between Common Threads classes, when I would see these students in the hallway, they would often grab my arm and tell me they could hardly wait to see how big their plants had grown. Watching their vegetables grow was truly remarkable to them, and for many of them, this was their first foray into "nature."

As cool as it was to see the plants growing, I didn't have much of a green thumb, and so I felt more excited about the cooking component. Each week, the students made a new dish, ranging from salmon with a homemade pesto sauce to a curried Indian peanut soup. I was so impressed with how well they fell into the role of chefs, adeptly measuring ingredients and chiffoning basil with expertise!

Common Threads ended up being a program I'd take a group of students to each fall, although I perennially wished I had the opportunity to teach cooking and gardening to *all* of my students, rather than just the 30 kids I could bring at the start of each school year. Many of the students I took on these trips later reported they'd decided they wanted to be a chef when they grew up (obviously as a direct result of having this experience), and I'm quite glad to say quite a few of the others went on to enroll in culinary arts classes in high school.

The more I saw what a difference it made to expose students to life-enhancing activities that were otherwise outside of the world they knew, the more I realized that cultivating these experiences was where I wanted to be spending my time. I knew the work I did as a therapist was incredibly impactful, and I sincerely believe a great deal of the issues plaguing inner city kids could be mitigated if we would provide them with more social/emotional and mental health services. But because there were not enough mental health providers to go around to supply the deep level of service these students deserved, I knew that exposing students to new opportunities like Common Threads was just as powerful, if not more so.

Just as I had done with my internship students back at Arnold, I began applying for more restaurant gift cards from downtown restaurants. And soon, I was taking as many groups as I could downtown. We followed a similar path to the one I'd taken with my students from Arnold: touring Northwestern's law school and ending up at one of the fine dining restaurants downtown that supported our venture, such as Quartino. However, the biggest challenge remained transportation.

Because Jonathan was located just blocks from the Chicago Transit Authority's "red line," it was easy for me and my fellow chaperone to walk with a small group of students from our school to the 95th Street red line stop, and to take the train all the way downtown, where it would drop us off within a few blocks of the

Northwestern campus. However, Thompson was located in an area I'd always thought of as an alcove: it was south and so far east that no major CTA lines went anywhere near it. As a result, we would have had to take multiple buses to get downtown—and even walking from Thompson to the bus would have been unsafe, as the neighborhood surrounding Thompson was a hotbed for gang activity.

I hated that I was able to take my Jonathan students on these amazing field trips, but my Thompson students were missing out. Even though Jonathan was ranked higher (according to test scores and other academic assessment measures) than Thompson, I felt it was important for *all* students to gain exposure to a college environment, and it was perhaps even more important for Thompson students to have such experiences, since they were less likely to get the opportunity anywhere else.

So, I developed a plan to take Thompson kids on a proper college trip, and over the course of a few months was able to put together enough money to pay for a trip to visit both a college and a top vocational high school, all via a school bus (since public transit wasn't an option).

One portion of the plan was inspired by the fact that my father is a principal at a vocational high school in Indiana – actually, in a town located not far from the Illinois/Indiana border. Growing up, I'd witnessed the remarkable things that can happen when students learn a vocational trade. Many of those who attended his school learned trades ranging from nursing to elementary education to welding to computer-aided design, and so much more. I've watched them build houses, learn how to cut hair as adeptly as any professional hair stylist, make all sorts of useful objects with 3D printers, and get training in law enforcement. Not all of the students end up pursuing into their professional lives the primary skill set they learned in high school. However, many do, and a large percentage of my dad's students leave high school with a job already lined up. In fact, many of his students make more money their first year out of high school than the average college graduate.

I knew exposing my students to a top tier vocational school like my father's could be life-changing, particularly for those who had interests and skills that aligned better with vocational trades (i.e., instead of steering them toward going to a traditional college). I started looking for similarly high quality Chicago area vocational schools. Sadly, I didn't find any. Technically speaking, there *were* a couple of schools offering some vocational programming, but none anywhere near as extensively as my father's school. And the schools I did find were known more as alternative schools, i.e., the type of schools where "problem kids" went when they weren't able to get into any other high school. These seemed to be a far cry from what I wanted to show my students, as a "vision of possibilities."

Then the thought occurred to me: *Why couldn't I take my students to visit my dad's school?* Knowing there was also a good quality college in my hometown, Valparaiso University, I could take my students to both the university and also to my dad's school in the same trip, thus maximizing the money spent on the bus.

FOURTEEN

. . .

As soon as I formed this plan, I became incredibly excited! Taking Arnold and Jonathan students to visit Northwestern law school had been terrific and eye-opening, but it wasn't the same as a trip to Valparaiso University (VU), for two reasons. One, VU had an actual undergraduate campus, which could be viewed as a much more tangible, immediate possibility for middle schoolers. (Attending Northwestern law school, while surely being feasible for any of my students who wished to go there, still seemed "far in the future" for the average eighth-grade student.)

And second, going to a campus located in Chicago was certainly convenient, but I loved the idea of taking my students on a trip out of state, away from the city life they were used to. Visiting VU would give them a better feel for a more traditional college experience. I had learned over time that exposing students to life outside of the neighborhood they were used to could be one of the most positively transformational experiences they could have. For so many of my students, not only were they not accustomed to leaving their neighborhood (even to go to downtown Chicago), but most of them didn't know anyone in their family or their neighborhood who had been to college. This may not seem like a big deal to someone whose family members have all attended and graduated from college, but it can be incredibly hard to break patterns that have been ingrained in families for generations.

For months, I worked diligently to plan the trip, coordinating with staff members from both VU and my dad's school. When the day finally arrived, I was on pins and needles. On the morning of our field trip, forty eighth graders and I, along with four staff members, piled into a school bus and traveled across the state border to head to Indiana. Our first stop was Valparaiso University. Now, VU normally only allows high school students to take "official" campus tours, but as I was apparently the first person to ever call them from a Chicago inner city school, because my mom worked at VU and pulled some strings, and because I begged and pleaded with the tour coordinator, they made an exception for my students.

Valparaiso University is a fairly small university (fewerthan five thousand students per year) whose campus seemed rather humble compared to the sprawling, gorgeous campus of Indiana University where I attended college. But for my students, having never set foot on an out of state college campus before, this was a whole new world.

Indeed, these often jaded eighth-grade students momentarily forgot to act cool as they excitedly pressed their faces to the cold windows of the bus. We filed off the bus and into an administration building, where we were to meet with our tour guides. The students walked around the building in awe, clearly impressed by the beautiful, modern look of everything, and also by the generally nicely-dressed college kids who were walking around in between classes.

Once our entire busload of people was split into smaller groups and each assigned a tour guide, off we went to explore the campus. My group walked through a classroom, and my students took a few minutes to sit in the chairs the college students used. They loved the modern, swiveling orange seats, and seemed to be having as much fun as if we had been visiting an arcade.

We next took a stroll through one of the cafeterias. The combination of the food options—everything from healthy choices to fast food to homemade-style hot meals—combined with seeing the college students walking around, independently "doing their own things" with friends and classmates, seemed to blow their minds. I loved knowing my students were picturing themselves going to a school like this and that their horizons were being expanded with every passing minute we spent at VU.

My small group also toured through more academic buildings, and each student seemed to be listening attentively as the tour guide talked about all of the course options each student had at VU, ranging from technology classes to music to meteorology.

We ended our tour by walking through the VU chapel, which I knew from past experience many people consider to be an architectural treasure with its many tallstained glass windows. When I was a young girl, my mother took my sister and me to hear Supreme Court Justice Sandra Day O'Connor speak at the chapel, which is one of my earliest memories. At the time, I was too young to truly understand much of O'Connor's talk, but, looking back as an adult, I appreciate the significance of having been there. I hoped my students would also look back on their day at VU with a similar sense of appreciation.

As we departed the campus, I could tell this would likely be the case. They didn't want to leave VU, and many exclaimed they were, no questions asked, going to attend college there. The sad reality was only a few of my students had a realistic shot at attending VU, since the vast majority of them had grades too low to qualify. Even my highest achieving students were handicapped somewhat, because being a "high achiever" at Thompson meant they were still a significant distance behind their North Side and suburban Chicago counterparts.

I also knew none of my students could have afforded to go to VU without a full-ride tuition, and the application process for financial aid was a huge obstacle in and of itself for many students. But I hoped perhaps *some* of them would make it to VU and that, at the least, the trip inspired them to see going to college as a very real possibility and no longer an abstract concept that wasn't an option for them.

Our next stop was my dad's school. As much as my students loved VU, I knew they would be equally as impressed with what they would see at this remarkable vocational school. When my students got off the bus to head into his school, my dad stood outside in the cold, greeting each and every one of them with a handshake. That action alone was something that was new to many of my students, who were used to adults showing more contempt toward them than respect.

At first, we all congregated in one classroom, as my dad introduced himself, his teachers, and some of the students who would be acting as tour guides that day. Our bunch again split into small groups, and each group eventually got a chance to see every classroom. This particular building held classes ranging from CAD (computer-aided design) to health sciences, and the vocational center also ran a few other vocational programs that were held at other satellite campuses.

My students got to don hard hats in the welding area, they played with the 3-D printer in the computer-aided design class, and they got to see themselves "live" on video in the videography class. In each room, they heard from students in the class about what they were learning and what they loved most about the course. At the end of the day, my students once again did not want to leave. Many of them told my dad on the way out the door, they couldn't wait to attend his school the following year, as high school freshman.

Again, it was unfortunate this wasn't a viable option for my students. My dad's school was located in Porter County in Indiana and was only available to students who lived in that county. But the most important takeaway, I believe, was how clearly their experience on this field trip turned my students on to new possibilities for their future, a mission I certainly felt grateful was accomplished.

Over the years I worked in CPS, I went on to take my students on a variety of field trips, ranging from other college tours to health centers to museums. Still, the day I took my Thompson students to VU and to my dad's school remains one of the favorite days of my lifetime. I *also* took my Jonathan students on the same field trip—VU and my father's vocational high school—a few months later, but they didn't experience the same thrill that my Thompson students had. Unlike at Thompson, many Jonathan students had parents who had attended college and many had siblings whom they had visited in college. It was more expected for these students to be aware of collegiate life, and thus the appeal and draw was not the same.

I was fascinated to see the difference in how students from my two schools responded so differently. I loved working with those at Jonathan, and, truthfully, my job there was exponentially easier than at Thompson, where I seemed to be constantly called upon to handle one crisis after another, every single day. In comparison, life at Jonathan was *much* easier, and I often saw my work there as a breath of fresh air, compared to the chaos at Thompson. Jonathan kids were still economically disadvantaged, compared to the average North Side student in Chicago, but they had a great deal of resources available to them (in comparison to Thompson students): a roof over their heads and food on the table, typically a loving family, safety and security, and role models who had stable jobs and college degrees. But the experience I had of the field trip with my Thompson students reminded me how much I loved working with those students who, in many ways, society had already given up on, and it solidified my commitment to serving children who had the greatest level of need.

FIFTEEN

· · ·

L ater that year, the documentary *Waiting for Superman* came out. I had received an invite to attend a pre-screening of the film, so I went with my husband and a fellow social worker friend. The movie delves into what is really happening in public schools across America, and explores the many ways in which the system is failing students, particularly low-income, minority students.

A big part of *Waiting for Superman* involves following the path of low-income teens in Washington, D.C. who apply to attend the SEED school. SEED was the country's first public boarding school for urban youth, and, since its inception in 1997, it has received national attention for the finding that a SEED graduate is three times more likely to graduate from college than a child with a similar background attending their neighborhood public school. More than 80 percent of SEED graduates are first-generation, college-bound students, and SEED graduates who do go to college earn $40,000 to $50,000 more annually than their peers. SEED is seen as a much higher quality option, education-wise, than most of the DC public schools, plus many families are attracted to the fact that SEED is residential, which brings with it many additional resources that wouldn't otherwise be available to students (www. SeedFoundation.com)

Washington, D.C. is known for being a highly segregated city, with a wide disparity between wealthy, predominantly white neighborhoods—where kids can attend high quality public schools—and low-income, predominantly black and Latino neighborhoods with subpar public schools. Throughout the film, we see the impact getting into SEED produces, as some families rejoice when their child is selected from the SEED lottery, while other families break down in tears when they find out their child was not selected. It pained me greatly to watch these scenes, and I remember thinking how unfair it was that it should be up to the luck of the draw whether or not a child receives an excellent education in a safe environment, or whether they must attend an overcrowded, understaffed school where few, if any children were achieving at grade level.

The film confirmed my feelings of anger toward the greater societal systems that I saw keeping the poor poorer, while providing more resources and opportunities to the wealthy, who already were light years ahead. Since working in CPS, I had become increasingly frustrated with the lack of quality educational options for students on the South Side of Chicago, and seeing this movie precipitated my desire to be able to more profoundly impact the lives of more students than I was able to do in my current role.

I was a product of public education, and my father is a principal at a public school in my hometown. So, I suppose it was natural that I'd always wanted to give the public school system the benefit of the doubt. In my adult life, I'd been a huge advocate for public education—but at the same time, I'd also come to see so many flaws in the system that didn't seem fixable.

I started spending more time brainstorming what other measures I could take. I came up with a lot of ideas for programming options that would help my students, and though I wanted to implement them all, I was limited in terms of both time and money. After taking my students on the uber-successful field trip to VU and the vocational school, one of the ideas I'd thought long and hard about was developing a nonprofit that would fund these types of trips. I knew visiting colleges could be a pivotal experience for any child, particularly one who has grown up in a world where college didn't seem like it was an option for them.

But the more I explored this route, the more I realized it just wasn't enough. There were so many issues that made success almost an impossibility for many of my students. Aside from those existing outside of school (homelessness, poverty, abuse, violence, etc.), I knew my students were also not getting the quality education they deserved. Collectively, this meant by the time a child was old enough to tour a university campus, it might be, in some ways, too late.

There were many reasons for this. South and West Side schools in Chicago paled in comparison to schools on the North Side, all of which were cleaner, more likely to be new or renovated, and simply nicer. It never seemed fair to me there could be such a large discrepancy in quality between schools in the same district that should be receiving equal treatment. But because there *was* a drastic difference, the North Side schools attracted a higher caliber of teacher, and they were also less likely to have an issue with teacher retention.

South Side schools, which sometimes felt like dilapidated jail cells to me, often presented as unpleasant atmospheres, and, coupled with the additional stressors associated with teaching in an inner city school, made for extremely challenging, less desirable work environments (when compared to the North Side schools), to say the least.

Additionally, as anyone who works in a large public school system can attest, there seem to be two main camps of teachers, though of course there are always exceptions: teachers who are young, full of energy and heart, and passionate about making a difference, and the older teachers—seasoned veterans who have been working there for a decade, or in some cases, for a *few* decades.

In my experience, though, I saw that some of these veteran teachers seemed to have lost their passion. And I certainly believe more than just "time" was the cause. I observed many South Side teachers and other school clinicians (e.g., school social workers, like myself) initially coming into the work ready to dive in, get their hands dirty and make a difference. They were idealistic and ready to do whatever it took to help their students succeed. But over time, the reality of the situation seemed to sink in—that is, they couldn't help but see and feel the heart-rending effects of the detrimental, unhealthy and destructive factors so many of their students had to face daily, both within the school and outside it in their homes and neighborhoods.

However, it's very likely that countless numbers of these teachers have eventually realized how many factors (including political and economic forces embedded in the prevailing institutional systems) were at play that kept inner city youth in a self-perpetuating cycle of intergenerational poverty and how challenging it was to break that cycle. It would be a demanding task for these teachers to truly meet the educational (let alone emotional) needs, even if there was just *one* child in each class who was facing such seemingly insurmountable obstacles, but there wasn't just one. Rather, in many cases, such as at Thompson, each and every child had a high level of need. As a result, the evidence I saw demonstrated to me that, without the necessary support provided in the critical areas mentioned above, by and large, South Side teachers became more and more drained.

I want to highlight the fact that there are hundreds of terrific, world-class teachers in CPS (I've had the honor of working alongside some of them) and also many outstanding administrators. I believe it's difficult to place the full onus of responsibility on the teachers for being "inadequate" in the classroom, when I believe so many of them go into the profession ready to dive in and change lives, only to become burned out by a system that doesn't equip them with the resources and backing they deserve. Even more importantly, I witnessed that CPS teachers often did not receive the respect they deserved for taking such a tiring, demanding job.

A couple of years into my job, the CTU (Chicago Teachers Union) warned that we'd possibly have to go on strike for a multitude of reasons. The union was protesting against what they felt was an unfair contract, mandatory furlough days that had left teachers without pay, and CPS's decision to cut numerous positions across the city. One of the biggest concerns they were facing was the new contract that would have given teachers less pay than before and taken away any cost of living increase they should have received. For months, the CTU had organized protest marches where thousands of CTU members, including me, spoke out against this unfair contract that would have hurt not just teachers, but students. Many parents also argued against the new contract, primarily for this reason.

The CTU did eventually decide to go on strike for the first time in 25 years, which meant no CTU member (basically all of the staff members at all of the schools with the exception of security, admin, and janitorial staff) was allowed to go to work. And if anyone *did* cross the picket line, they would lose their right to be in the union. As such, children did not go to school during this time, and parents had to find alternative places to take their children for daycare during the school day, since many of them had to go to work.

With more than 400,000 kids in CPS, this strike threw a wrench into the entire city of Chicago, since an equal number (or more) of parents were affected by this decision, as well. On the day the strike began, instead of reporting to their job as normal, CTU members instead showed up at the picket lines. But not me.

At the time of the strike, I was training for my sixth marathon and was set to run the Chicago Marathon for what would be my fourth time. After work one day, I went for an easy 9-mile training run, and I recall it being gorgeous that afternoon, as I ran in the sunshine along the path alongside Lake Michigan. My mom had broken her foot the day before, and as I ran, I was thinking about my mom and how I felt so badly for her. My plan was to pick up some food I knew she'd like and to drive to Indiana to see her the following day. As I kept running and formulating this plan in my head, I started to feel pain in my right foot. I kept running through it for a few miles, thinking it would go away (as "runner's pain" often does), but it did not subside and instead got worse. Eventually, the aching was so bad I had to stop. Being a few miles from home without any money to call a cab (and pre-Uber days), I called a friend to come pick me up.

I explained the situation, and we drove to a neighborhood urgent care clinic. To my dismay, the doctors there said I had fractured my foot and could no longer run—no running *at all*—for the next few months, and no marathon! I was given a boot to wear to stabilize my foot while I walked, and told to avoid, as much as possible, even walking or standing until I was completely healed. I had truly been looking forward to the marathon for months and was devastated I wasn't able to run it, especially since I'd already invested so much of my time, energy and money into preparing for the race.

However, the one silver lining to come out of my injury was that I had a legitimate excuse not to go on strike with the rest of my CTU comrades. And I'd like to clarify why I'm say this. *Striking is not a pleasant experience.* Everyone I knew in the CTU was dreading spending their days walking in circles, holding protest signs and yelling all day—and all the while, *not* getting a paycheck. For every day the CTU was on strike, those days would have to be made up somehow over the course of that year, since CPS students still had a legal right to an education and the school system had to provide a set amount of school days each year.

Teachers knew the strike could be over in a couple days *or it* could last a few months. Not only did nobody want to lose their summer vacation (which would happen if they had to continue work through the summer to make up for the lost days), but many teachers lived paycheck to paycheck, and to go on strike represented a huge financial struggle for them.

The boot on my foot exempted me from the typical strike activities, but I'd heard from CTU friends about what that particular strike experience was like. While many Chicago citizens supported the strike, there were many who did not. My friends reported hecklers driving by and telling them to stop complaining and get back to work, as well as other disrespectful remarks and gestures. Actually, I had experienced similar situations myself, during the summer leading up to the strike. It was not uncommon for me to be talking to someone I barely knew—e.g., someone at a friend's BBQ—who would make remarks to me like, "Who do you think you are for going on strike? How greedy! It's sickening! Teachers don't work enough hours as it is!"

Many people seemed to be under the impression that because they're taxpayers, they have a right to place demands on teachers and believe they understand what it takes to be a teacher in CPS. I would explain to them the strike was about so much more than fair pay—it was about how teachers were not given the basic necessities they needed to be effective teachers.

For example, one of the requests from the CTU was for teachers to receive their students' textbooks on the *first* day of school, rather than receiving them weeks, if not months into the school year (which, believe it or not, was common). Just stop and ask yourself: Is this truly worthy of being considered an arguable demand, asking that the books students use to learn arrive when the school year starts? Such an occurrence would never happen in a wealthier suburban school district.

Another issue the CTU was fighting for involved class sizes. In many South and West Side schools, the class sizes were often *twice or more* what the law dictated they should be. However, with the schools being asked to make budget cuts each year, the administrators didn't see any other way around this.

One year at Thompson, I recall a fifth-grade classroom having over 50 students in one class. They eventually were able to hire another teacher to help out, but for the first two months of the year, students were sitting on the windowsill, since there weren't enough desks and chairs to go around.

When the strike ended after 8 days, the CTU had negotiated a new contract with CPS that included educators barely receiving any of the contract items we had been asking for, and in fact ended up working longer hours for less pay! The entire experience was very disheartening for me and many CTU members, who went back to work feeling less empowered than before, and instead, beaten down from experiencing the seemingly continual vitriol that had been spewed at the teachers across the city.

SIXTEEN

• • •

Unfortunately, the strike paled in comparison to what teachers had to go through on a daily basis. CPS teachers were used to teaching in classrooms without enough school supplies to go around and with students who regularly came to school embroiled in serious, oftentimes high-risk or life-threatening matters—at home, in their neighborhoods and at school—that clearly had a significant negative impact on their ability to learn.

Dealing with trauma outside the school environment meant that many students came to school angry. A significant part of the job of many CPS teachers was not only instructing students on academic subjects, but also managing often extreme behavior issues. In a school like Thompson, it was normal for fights to break out multiple times per hour in a single classroom, which obviously completely impeded the teacher's ability to teach the rest of the class. Whenever this happened, if the student's behavior was too difficult to handle, he or she would be sent directly to the main office.

According to Paul Tough, the best-selling author of *How Children Succeed: What Works and Why*:

> *"Nationally, African American students are suspended three times as often as white students. In Chicago high schools, 27% of students who live in the city's poorest neighborhoods received an out of school suspension during the 2013-2014 school year, as did 30% of students with a reported personal history of abuse or neglect. 60% of Chicago's out of school suspensions are for infractions that didn't involve violence or even a threat of violence but rather were for being defiant or disruptive. This type of response is not an expression of a bad attitude or a defiant personality as it is from a poorly regulated stress-response system. These types of behaviors are symptoms of a child's inability to control impulses, de-escalate confrontations, and manage anger and other strong feelings—all self regulation issues that can usually be traced to impaired executive-function development in early childhood. In Chicago, high school students whose grades are in the lowest GPA quartile are 4x more likely to be suspended than students whose grades are in the top quartile"* (2013).

Though sending a misbehaving student was often a necessity in order for the teacher to continue instructing the rest of the class, such occurrences unfortunately sent the message to students that acting out led to a "free day" spent in the principal's office. Many teachers also seemed to lack the proper training to know how to appropriately deal with student behavior issues, and it was common for me to walk down the hall and hear teachers screaming at their class at the top of their lungs. I hated hearing this, as I knew that being berated in this manner was *never* going to help a student behave more appropriately and, in fact, would only serve to push them further away from the teacher and what she or he wanted them to do.

I also began noticing how so many staff members I'd worked with had serious health issues, most of which they (and I) attributed to the stress of working in CPS. It was commonplace for teachers to take medications for anxiety and/or depression, and being saddled with these mental health issues also caused some of them to miss a great deal of school. I knew quite a few teachers who'd had to take a sick leave due to their anxiety or depression, whenever it had become so debilitating they temporarily could not return to school.

I was technically one of three mental health professionals in each building—there was also a school counselor and psychologist—so according to CPS, they had provided "enough" mental health providers for each school. However, I was the only one of these three clinicians who actually provided counseling. The school psychologist was assigned to 3-5 different schools or more, and their sole responsibility was testing students to determine if they qualified for an individualized education program (IEP)—that is, they did not provide counseling.

The school counselor was also the school case manager, which means they were tasked with running IEP meetings, and helping eighth graders get into high school. With me as the only person in each of my schools who actually provided counseling, this meant that not only was I tasked with individual, group and crisis counseling for students, but I was the one *teachers* came to, as well, when they were in distress. I often found myself in a position where I had gone to a teacher's classroom to speak to them about a particular student, only to find myself pulled into a discussion about how stressed out that teacher was and how it was impacting not only his or her mental health, but also their physical health and personal relationships.

Indeed, many teachers shared with me how much the job stress was putting a strain on their marriages, and the divorce rate for CPS teachers seemed higher than average. But what was even more noticeable was the rate of health issues these teachers suffered from. Aside from depression and panic attacks, it seemed everywhere I looked I saw a teacher who had ulcers or who'd experienced a recent stroke or heart attack. According to the teachers who were impacted by these maladies, these health issues were brought on both by the immense pressure they were under from the CPS administration and also from the shifts in federal guidelines that basically translated into teachers being instructed to spend their time "teaching to the test," instead of using innovative and creative approaches to teach their students.

When I spoke to senior teachers who had been in CPS for many decades, they all expressed the same feeling of discouragement, saying that teaching simply wasn't enjoyable anymore. They felt bogged down in bureaucracy and regulations which kept them from providing more effective instruction and support to their students. In fact, nearly all the teachers I spoke to, both young and old, said they would never encourage a young person to go into the teaching profession.

I found this to be troubling, to think the field of education—which had already gone downhill so far over the past decade, particularly in CPS—had reached the point when it would be truly hard to attract quality people to the culturally essential field of teaching. Research studies have shown many of the country's brightest young people are choosing other professions over teaching, presumably because of low pay and a lack of respect. One survey of college freshmen from UCLA's Cooperative Institutional Research Program found that the number of students who say they will major in education had reached its lowest point in 45 years with only 4.2% planning to major in education (2016). It's truly disheartening to imagine a world where the number of qualified, enthusiastic people wanting to become teachers has decreased to nearly zero.

The job stress at Thompson and Jonathan was so bad it often had repercussions far worse than ulcers and stress. One day at Jonathan, a teacher had a heart attack and died in her classroom, in the middle of teaching her students. This teacher was quite young—only in her early forties—and had indeed been under a great deal of stress, having taken on a new job at Jonathan, while also going through a divorce. However, it's indicative of the stressful atmosphere I've been describing here. And certainly, this event was incredibly traumatic for the students in her classroom who witnessed this happening, as well as for everyone else in the school (including her fellow teachers).

Being called into the role of pseudo-therapist for my fellow staff members was a duty I was more than happy to do, as I knew the importance of providing these teachers with an outlet for them to express themselves and their frustrations. But it became very hard on me, as time went on, feeling the weight of these teachers' grief and emotional stress on my shoulders, in addition to the weight I carried from my students. The fact is, social workers and others in the helping professions can very easily suffer from what is called "compassion fatigue," otherwise known as secondary trauma or vicarious trauma, which is chronic stress taken on by those who work in helping professions.

For any staff member working closely with students who'd experienced such intense trauma, it was easy to begin to take on some of it, which could affect us internally. I was easily susceptible to this, and it became increasingly harder to keep up my typically sunny demeanor.

A friend urged me to talk with my doctor about taking anti-anxiety medication to deal with the stress. I finally went and did get a prescription from my doctor to take "when needed." However, I found the medication did nothing to alleviate my stress. By this point, I knew leaving CPS was the only route that would truly help me start to relieve all the pressure, strain and anxiety, so I could begin feeling like myself again. I also recognized I never wanted to become one of those who'd become complacent in their job, or destroy my own health and sanity in the process of simply doing my job.

It hadn't taken me long to notice almost all first-year CPS staff members would come into their respective roles bright-eyed and idealistic, excited about the chance to educate young minds. But within a few months or even less, I could see the weariness on these new teacher's faces. Over the span of a few years, sadly, this passion and idealism almost always seemed to be sucked dry.

As difficult as these interactions were for me to deal with— and as much as they began to wear on me personally—I still truly enjoyed my job. I loved the kids I worked with, and though the majority of the time it felt as if I wasn't ever doing enough, I relished the occasional moment where my students would have breakthroughs. During these mini-leaps of progress, it would feel like we took an important and vital step forward.

Still, in time I started to wonder whether there was a way for me to continue working with students, but to step into a role that would allow me to have a much greater impact on more students at once.

SEVENTEEN

• • •

For a long time, I had wanted to go back to school to get my second Master's degree in Educational Leadership, also referred to as a "Type 75" degree. This particular degree would enable me to work as a school principal or to take a leadership position within the social work department.

After recently getting divorced, I decided it was the time for me to finally pursue this degree. My father—once a teacher, himself—had transitioned into the role of school principal, so I had seen firsthand how many more students my father was able to impact while working from an administrative leader's capacity. I was unsure whether I had the fortitude to be a principal in CPS. Although that was the population of students I most wanted to serve, I saw how exhausted and miserable many CPS principals were. I considered the possibility of working as a vice principal in CPS for a couple of years and then becoming a principal in the suburbs, where the quality of life would be exponentially higher *and* where I could actually do my job. But deep down, I didn't want to go to the suburbs, as I had always been drawn to working with the most vulnerable populations.

When I trained for my first marathon, I raised money for the Afghan Women's Organization (AWO), a charity many of my friends and family didn't quite understand. "Why are you drawn to run in support of people you don't even know, halfway across the world?" I was asked way more than once.

Having grown up hearing from my parents about the plight of women living in underdeveloped African nations, the AWO felt like a cause I'd like to contribute to and a demographic that would benefit from any assistance. I had always been outraged by social injustices—especially those impacting women and children—and the fact that many Afghan women live without basic human rights many Westerners take for granted only fueled my desire to help. A 2010 *TIME Magazine* cover featured an 18-year-old Afghan woman who had her nose and ears cut off by a Taliban commander for escaping from her abusive in-laws. Stories like hers made me want to advocate on their behalf.

Similarly, while there are many exceptions to this scenario, most children growing up in the suburbs of Chicago have an abundance of resources that are just not available to students living on the South or West Sides of the city. These suburban kids were used to living in safe homes and safe neighborhoods and did not have to walk to school past dead bodies, discarded drug needles or used condoms. They didn't have to wonder where their next meal was coming from or whether they would hear gunshots at night. Instead, suburban students were surrounded by a community where it was expected that most of them would attend college and enter the workforce in a more assured manner.

I researched a number of schools in my area that provided the degree, and I chose an online program, so I wouldn't have to spend hours every week traveling to the suburbs. I had accumulated a healthy amount of student loan debt from my bachelor's and first master's degrees, and knew there was no way I wanted to add on more debt. Therefore, I made the decision to pay for the degree out of pocket and forked over a few thousand dollars for the first semester. After ordering my textbooks, I excitedly dove into my first class, Education Law.

I loved learning about the legalities of being a principal, running a school, and about previous education lawsuits that had set precedent for current law. I'd gone straight from undergrad into grad school to get my MSW and then had worked in the field for about four years, before I'd decided to get my MA in Educational Leadership. After finishing my MSW, I was tired of taking tests and studying, but the four-year hiatus from classwork had given me a second wind. I really enjoyed the law class and surprised myself at how much I looked forward to, not just learning concepts, ideas, systems and applications of these that were new to me, but also to writing about such.

As much as I loved the content of the class, I also think part of my exuberance was due to the immediate gratification it brought me. I had always been someone who liked seeing results and feeling a sense of accomplishment, but in my role in CPS, it was rare I ever truly felt accomplished. There was always so much more work to do, and no matter what I did over the course of the day, I always felt behind, because the level of need was so great. My master's classes afforded me the opportunity to finish an assignment (which in and of itself felt like a small victory), and then, once the paper was returned to me, it brought a sense of satisfaction I hadn't realized I'd been missing for so long.

Though all of the classes weren't as interesting as the law class, overall I really enjoyed the program, even if it *did* take an exorbitant amount of time. The program was comprised of two years of classes, plus during the second year I also took a practicum, during which I worked closely with one of the principals at my schools. I was assigned to take on a variety of administrative projects, in order to get "practice" being a school principal. The classes, readings, papers and practicum assignments added a couple dozen extra hours to my already busy week, but I knew I would one day be glad to have this degree.

For one of my program's final papers, I had to design my own school, and there was no question in my mind—it would be a boarding school. The idea had been floating around in my head for years, and after Arne Duncan left CPS to head to D.C. to work for President Obama, it seemed clear I couldn't wait around for someone else to spearhead this project. It still seemed like a nebulous concept, a dream that might come true "one day down the road in a land far, far away," rather than something concrete, realistic and actually attainable in the somewhat near future. But the more I spent time crafting the vision for my "dream" boarding school, the more fired up I became. Occasionally, I'd let myself bask in the vision and think: *Maybe it's in the cards for me, after all?* Though I didn't announce it publicly, a big part of why I pursued the MA in Educational Leadership was because of this deep, burning desire to build a boarding school. I knew having this experience, background and advanced degree would lend credibility to me as a leader.

A year into my MA program, I'd started to feel rumblings of frustration and a "stuckness" I just couldn't shake. Something about my work didn't feel right. However, at first, I couldn't put my finger on it. I truly *did* love working with my students and their families, even though it was an incredibly difficult, draining and emotionally taxing job. Still, for the first few years, I was so passionate about the work, I assumed I would stay there until my retirement, decades later. But what emerged was the sense that something was missing, and I knew I needed to figure out what it was.

One spring day as I was driving to Thompson, I decided to put this question to the people who knew me best, to see what their take was. After I parked my car in the parking lot at school, I sent a quick text to my family members: "I think I need to switch careers. Is there anything you've always thought I would be good at?"

Throughout the day, I thought about the activities I'd always loved to do and the work I'd known I was great at, in an attempt to find an intersection of the two. After I got home from work that day, I took a long walk along Lake Michigan, during which I received two text messages nearly at the same time—one from my mom and one from my sister. They both told me I should be a life coach.

For years, I had been told I would be an excellent life coach, but I had always brushed it off. *What the heck is a life coach, anyway?* I'd often wondered. I wasn't entirely sure what that job entailed, but I knew I was certainly not an expert at life! So I'd laughed off the idea that anyone would pay me to be their life coach. But for some reason on this particular sunny afternoon, the idea felt right.

I did some investigation and realized life coaching sounded very similar to what I had already been doing—pro bono—for years, although just not realizing it. My entire adult life, I'd found myself in situations where I would be at a party talking to a stranger, and, after our discussion, the person would thank me for helping them to change their perspective and thereby their life. It *did* always seem to go beyond the role I'd played at work as a social worker—that is, I wasn't giving therapy as I would to the CPS students, but was asking potent, thought-provoking questions that inspired these people I'd innocently encounter to take a close, hard look at their lives and how their thoughts, feelings, beliefs and actions impacted both themselves and the world, as well as how their mindset, physical health, relationships, and goals were all interconnected.

Walking along the lake, it finally hit me this could be the perfect path for me. I had recently spent some time getting clear on the various criteria that were non-negotiables for me in my "ideal" work role (e.g., I wanted to make a difference, work from home, have a flexible schedule, etc.) and life coaching did fit the bill for all of them. So, despite already working full-time at a highly stressful job, being immersed in the tasks required for finishing my second year in the MA program, *and* being in the middle of my practicum, I decided, *What the heck… why not start a business, too?*

I had wanted to be an entrepreneur since I was a little girl, and I now felt ready to take the plunge. I began doing as much research as I could regarding how to start a business. Ultimately, I launched a life coaching business and created a podcast, for which I'd interview inspiring people who had accomplished amazing things in their lives. And though I was incredibly busy, I absolutely loved it, and learned how to apply the work I was doing as a coach to my work with my students. I was still practicing according to traditional therapy models, but I began integrating more strengths-based, solutions-focused coaching principles into my work, as well. To a large extent, I had always done this, but I started to really focus on helping my students get excited about their futures, rather than simply rehashing the past.

I found that, in time, one of my favorite activities to do with my coaching clients *and* my students was lead them through an exercise that helped them articulate their core values. The fact is, when I'd walked myself through this exercise, I'd come to a sobering realization. Though my work in CPS allowed me to be of service to others, which was a core value for me, another of my top values was that of accomplishment: taking action that resulted in my seeing both progress and results. Due to the nature of being an inner-city school social worker, I'd realized I would never truly feel the sense of accomplishment I needed.

After going into social work to make a difference, it was starting to wear on me that I'd rarely ever felt I was doing enough. I knew if I continued to work in CPS, I would love the work for many reasons. Nonetheless, there would always be something missing that would keep me from being truly fulfilled. I knew in that moment I would not be able to stay at CPS much longer. And though I didn't speak about this publicly, I planned to work another year while growing my coaching practice, with the idea I'd leave CPS to work full-time on my business. At the same time, I also relished this plan because I secretly wanted to build the boarding school of my dreams.

EIGHTEEN

• • •

At the beginning of that calendar year I had started to make vision boards with many of my student groups. Because so many crises often got in the way of me seeing my groups as regularly as I wanted, this particular project took some of my groups longer than others to finish. One of the groups had a handful of seventh-grade boys in it who, surprisingly, were quite excited about the prospect of making vision boards. This was despite my concern they might think it was too "girly" to cut out words and pictures from magazines. And though most of the boys cut out pictures of supermodels and sports cars, the vision of one of the boys in my group was different. Niazi "Ryan" Banks had a vision board that was *full* of inspirational words, like "the power of the possible" and "the world's greatest starts with a single step."

Though Ryan had a difficult life, he had always stood out from the crowd, given he was the class clown *and* one of the happiest boys ever to walk the halls of Thompson, despite his difficult home life. He had ADHD and often got in trouble for being silly and talking during class, but he was otherwise a really great kid. Ryan loved making people laugh and would often bound into my office, Kramer-style, flying into the room in a whirlwind of energy. He'd always lead with, "Hey, Ms. G.!"

Ryan would often excitedly ask me what I was up to and if he could have some counseling time. Initially, I would ask if his teacher knew where he was, to make sure he had indeed received permission to be out of his classroom—to which his answer often varied. If he didn't, I would send Ryan back to his classroom, ignoring his playful begging and pleading for me to let him stay to talk.

On the days when we had one-on-one social work time together, he loved to learn about places he'd pick out on the globe that was sitting on my desk. When I first started working with Ryan, I was shocked he couldn't place Chicago or even the United States on the globe, although I soon realized that, sadly, this was commonplace for many students. Over time, I taught Ryan about geography and the culture, climate and terrain of different countries around the world. He would regularly come in, find a country on the globe, and we would look it up on the internet to learn intriguing facts about that country. Ryan soon accumulated a mental list of dozens of countries he wanted to visit.

Before leaving my office, he would always put on his head a black and red Mohawk hat I had in my "treasure" drawer. One of my dad's students had knitted the cap by hand, and Ryan had immediately taken to it. But I told him I wasn't able to just *give* him the hat, but that, just like the other students who I worked with, he would have to earn it through "good behavior reports" from his classroom teacher.

The next few months were incredibly hectic, as there were more crises than ever before. One of the cases involved a fourth-grade boy at Thompson who'd witnessed a double homicide in his family's living room, and his parents sent him to school the next day. Now, any adult I know who has found him- or herself in that type of traumatic situation would have not only taken off work the following day, but most likely would have taken a leave of absence to attend counseling, in order to cope with what would most assuredly be a bout with PTSD. But it was common for South

Side parents to send their students back to school immediately after something like this had happened, which I believe came from a combination of inadequate child development knowledge—i.e., not understanding how the child is impacted by witnessing such a violent tragedy—and, typically, a lack of appropriate childcare, thereby nullifying the option of having the student stay home.

However, this case was different. When I went to take this boy from his class to speak to him, he'd been told he was sworn to secrecy about who the killer was—and then immediately told me the name of the person who allegedly committed the double homicide! However, he didn't tell me the person's full name, but rather used the street name the kids in the neighborhood called him. Had I gotten a full name from the child I would of course have been obligated to report it to the police, but a nickname didn't give me as much of a leg to stand on.

But I also was worried the young boy might tell his family members (the ones who were helping to cover up the killer's identity) he had told me this person's name. This put me in a very dangerous position, as the life of anyone who knew the killer's identity could be in jeopardy. I immediately called my social work manager to talk about the predicament, and she said she'd speak to the CPS law department about the case. I was advised to take extra precautions when I was at that school, and if I wanted to abstain from working at Thompson for another week—until things "blew over"—I could work from my other school, instead. Though it's strange to say, thankfully, within a week, I had new crises on my mind . . . and whether or not my safety was still in jeopardy, I had mentally moved onto my next case.

Unfortunately, situations like this were not outside the norm. Numerous times before, I'd had to face instances during which my safety had been put in jeopardy. However, familiarity with such occurrences didn't make them any more comforting.

Before I knew it, the end of the school year was almost upon us. As much as I loved my students, I was greatly looking forward to the arrival of summer vacation and a chance to decompress from a long, stressful stretch of work. The last week in May, the NATO

Summit had arrived in Chicago, which ended up impacting me in an unexpected way. I lived in the South Loop, just south of downtown Chicago, which was right in the middle of the planned protests for the summit. One of my good friends was working as a nurse at a nearby hospital, and, because the planned strikes were going to shut down the streets around her hospital, I told her she could stay at my place. There wasn't much room in my small apartment, so to give her some space, my boyfriend and I headed to the suburbs for the weekend to get away from the craziness of the NATO Summit's arrival.

After a late evening spent golfing and going out to dinner, the next morning we took advantage of the quiet suburban morning and slept in. I put on the TV in our hotel room to check the weather and noticed the ticker along the bottom of the screen that mentioned a young boy had been shot and killed near Thompson. I remarked how I hoped it wasn't someone from my school and started thinking about heading back to the city to address the work I had to do when I got home.

As we were packing our bags to leave, my phone rang, and I saw it was Dr. Leonard, the vice principal. It was odd for her to call on a Sunday morning, but I didn't put two and two together until she spoke the words out loud: "Ms. G.., one of our kids was shot and killed last night. It was Niazi Banks."

"What?" I asked her to repeat the name, because I didn't know of any students by that name.

She repeated, "Niazi Ryan Banks."

I had forgotten Niazi was Ryan's given name.

I broke down and cried so loudly that the hotel staff came to the door to make sure I was ok. From there on, everything become a blur. John drove us back to the city, while I sent texts to my coworkers who knew Ryan to notify them about what had happened. Everyone was in shock, as Ryan was a beloved student at Thompson and at his previous schools, where his teachers and social worker still remembered him fondly. When we arrived back home in the South Loop, the NATO summit was in full effect, and I hazily watched as thousands of protesters marched beneath my building on South Michigan Avenue.

Aside from the news ticker that morning, there would be no mention of Ryan's death in the newspaper or on TV at all that week. To me, his being killed by gun violence was the utmost tragedy, but to the rest of Chicago, it was just another South Side shooting. Having news coverage of his death would not have made the situation any better, but it angered me to my core that the loss of a young black boy was not deemed "worthy" of making the news. Sure, the NATO Summit was the main focal point that weekend, but I felt strongly that had it been a white girl on the North Side who died in a shooting, it would have been front page news. On top of my shock and grief, I was enraged that it seemed as if nobody cared.

The next morning, I got up earlier than normal and left the house before 6 a.m. to head for school. There was a meeting scheduled, which would be attended by me, the school principals, the teachers who worked closely with Ryan, and members of the CPS crisis team, during which we were to talk about how to handle Ryan's death with the rest of the students and the school staff. As the main mental health professional at the school, I was used to being the point person for a crisis like this—I had done it many times before—and I was expected to do so again, for this case. But this crisis was different, and I was so personally distraught, I didn't know how I could possibly put aside my own grief to counsel students and staff. Thankfully, many of the teachers in attendance at the meeting spoke up to mention how close they knew I had been with Ryan, and the crisis team decided they would provide me with some backup.

That week continued to be a blur, as I did my best to counsel students and staff, but I felt as if I was walking through quicksand. I was truly grateful for the support from the crisis team, but many of the students I worked with regularly were also close to Ryan, and I wanted to be there for them. My office filled with dozens of students filtering in and out over the course of each day, joining the circle of students who had gathered to share stories about Ryan, and to cry, certainly, as well as to laugh (since Ryan was all about getting people to laugh).

We made cards to send to Ryan's family and a banner to hang in the seventh grade hallway, where students signed their name on it and wrote about their memories of Ryan. I had other students I needed to see, as well, but crises always came first. In addition to providing grief counseling to the best of my ability, I also had been in contact with Ryan's aunt about how to handle his funeral arrangements. I had never been in touch with her before Ryan's death, but she moved in with the family that week to take care of everyone. Understandably, all of the family members were in such grief, they could hardly conceive of how to plan a funeral, let alone how to pay for one. I had never planned a funeral before either, but I felt inspired to figure it out to help the family.

Planning a funeral is never a pleasant occasion, but I soon found out how much more challenging it is for a low-income family. I hadn't before realized that many simply don't have a funeral for their lost loved ones at all, because they can't afford it. Even more shocking to me, I found many of the deceased don't have a headstone, simply because of the expense. I learned there are special cemeteries where the poor are buried, with special sections for those who can't afford headstones.

I was appalled by the fact this could happen to Ryan, and I made phone calls all over the city, trying to find ways to help pay for the funeral. I eventually located a program that helped provide funeral expenses for people who'd died due to gun violence, which ended up helping out Ryan's family greatly. The headstone was another matter, but that ended up taking longer to work out.

We had recently found out more information about Ryan's death, although some of the details were still fuzzy. When he was killed, it was a warm Saturday night and he had been playing with his younger brother, Caleb, right around the corner from his house. Police alleged Ryan was caught "in a volley of bullets."

Many of the teachers were concerned there might be retaliation . . . not just in the neighborhood, but at the funeral. When I first heard about the notion of funeral retaliation, I was utterly floored—in my mind, there was no way people would actually bring guns into a funeral at a church to start shooting. But I was quickly educated about how intense gang retaliation could be. I was told a rival gang member will sometimes show up and shoot bullets into the deceased person's dead body lying there in the coffin, as a sign of disrespect—like spitting on someone's grave, but worse—and also to send a clear message to others that their gang was not to be messed with.

Though I was right to be wary about this, thankfully there was no violence at Ryan's funeral. But it was still one of the most difficult funerals I've ever had to attend. The dilapidated building in which it was held was located in a part of town so full of abandoned, boarded up buildings that I had to circle the block three times before I could locate the actual building. It didn't appear to have been used in many years, so I had inadvertently passed it the first two times I drove by.

In addition, at that point I was completely wrecked from the previous three weeks. I felt physically, mentally and emotionally exhausted, and longed for summer break to arrive, so I could take a break from dealing with trauma, day in and day out. Seeing Ryan's body in the casket was even more gut wrenching that I could have anticipated, and the undertaker's "preparation" was such that the small shell of a person lying in the casket looked nothing like Ryan (at least to me). I have vague memories of giving a hug to Ryan's aunt Brigette, who thanked me for my help planning the funeral, and I recall staying a few minutes after the service, before heading back to school.

Looking back, I recall that I left as quickly as I did, not just because I felt like my head was going to implode, but because other crises awaited me back at my schools. I was lucky enough to have gotten permission to take an hour out of my day to attend the funeral, something most teachers weren't able to do, since they didn't have anyone to cover their classes.

After the funeral, I stayed in close touch with Ryan's aunt, and she kept me up to date on how the family was doing in the aftermath. Sadly, Ryan's grandmother passed away just a couple of weeks later. Given that occurrence, it was good that Brigette had moved in, so she could take care of the household. One of the biggest challenges their family faced was living at the same residence where Ryan had been killed and having to walk down the steps every day where Ryan had taken his last breaths. A family with the financial means to do so would have no doubt moved as soon as possible, but this wasn't an option for Ryan's family. They would eventually move to a slightly safer part of town, but it would not be until many years after Ryan's death, when their request for public housing had finally gone through.

NINETEEN

· · ·

Over a year and a half later, I was surprised to run across an article by famed *Chicago Tribune* columnist, John Kass, who wrote about Ryan. He referred to him as "Peanut" Banks, which he had heard was a neighborhood nickname for Ryan, although Ryan's aunt and friends claim they'd never heard him go by that name before. A passage in John's column stuck out to me:

> "But his death on May 19, 2012 didn't make big news in Chicago. It was crowded out by the ceremony and spectacle of the NATO Summit, and what the mayor and the police chief were doing, and what the Occupy protesters and the anarchists were planning. "Politicians didn't read his eulogy. No White House Cabinet official declared that Peanut's death would be a 'line in the sand.' There were no grand speeches, no horde of national news reporters. That little boy with a squirrel on his shirt wasn't a national symbol of anything. Peanut fell below Chicago's notice like a stone."

I was so thankful to see John calling attention to Ryan's death and for saying what I had thought all along. I found his email address and reached out to thank him for writing such a great piece in memory of Ryan. Given John is a well-known journalist whose column I had been reading for years, I hadn't expected to hear back from him. I was shocked when I received an email response from his assistant that John wanted to learn more about me. I got on the phone with his assistant and told him a bit about myself, what I did as a school social worker, and about my relationship with Ryan. They later asked me if I would be willing to be interviewed for a story about Ryan. I immediately felt honored they'd asked, yet also hesitant.

A couple of years prior, I had been interviewed by the *Chicago Sun-Times* for the Letters to Santa program I had helped bring to Thompson, and I was misquoted as having said, "They are very needy kids" who are lacking for both presents and "even necessities like underwear." Though my statement was an accurate assessment of the prevailing conditions for many students' "experience" of Christmas, my words were taken out of context, and it came across to some students at Thompson as though I was being condescending. After that incident especially, and due to other experiences I'd had working with low-income students, I learned that none of them ever wanted to be actually labeled as "poor" or in need.

I'll never forget the day I walked into one of the eighth-grade classrooms the day the article had come out. The principal was so proud of the article and had made a copy for each of the students in the class. But the students were far from proud, and some of them hurled names at me as I entered the room. Caught off guard, I felt quite hurt by their words and attitudes, even though I tried not to take it too personally. I knew not allowing oneself to feel poor was a defense mechanism some of the students employed in order to not feel weak in an environment where they had to safeguard what little they did have.

I was also worried that if I spoke too honestly about the problems I'd observed at CPS, my boss or even someone higher up than her in CPS would come down on me, and I didn't want my job to be on the line. But John's assistant dissuaded my concern, assuring me they would be very careful about how the article was written, so no students, parents or anyone at CPS could be offended. We set up a time to meet at Sayat Nova, the Armenian restaurant around the corner from the *Chicago Tribune* building where John worked. When they arrived at the restaurant, I was impressed with how kind and compassionate they both were, bending over backwards to make sure I was comfortable.

John told stories about when he was a young beat reporter and was assigned to the south side of Chicago and how he cared deeply about inner city kids. I strongly objected to having my photograph taken, because I didn't want the article to be about me—I wanted it to be about Ryan. However, they insisted on taking a couple of photos, saying they probably wouldn't use them. Lunch was on them and I ordered a hummus plate, but hardly took more than a bite, as I focused on telling Ryan's story.

A few weeks later, the article was published in the *Chicago Tribune*, and it was quite surreal to see my name and Ryan's listed in an article by a journalist whose articles I had been reading since I was in high school. I came from a family of newspaper readers, and John Kass had been a household name. As nervous as I had been, he did a great job with the piece. I bought multiple copies of the paper that morning so I could give a copy to my family members, and I also took a copy to Ryan's aunt, so his family could read it, too.

At this point in the school year, I had been wavering back and forth on whether I was going to be able to continue working in CPS another year. I loved my students so much and hoped that my replacement would have sufficient drive, passion and dedication to give the students what I'd come to sense they needed. I also had the gnawing feeling there was so much more for me to be doing, or there was another path I should be taking that would allow me to help students on a much broader, more impactful level.

I was tired of being involved in horrific cases—like an 8-year-old girl being forced to watch her mom, a prostitute, have sex in front of her—*and* having DCFS do nothing about it. I was scared by the fact that, although I was still positively emotionally connected with my students, I had begun to learn how to be somewhat emotionally detached at the same time—especially from difficult cases—because on some unconscious level, my body and brain knew that was the only way for me to survive dealing with what I was so often facing.

I was tired of seeing one of my favorite students missing over four months of school, due to constant lice breakouts at her home, knowing she would be so far behind she would never catch up. In this particular student's case, it was not expected she would be graduating high school anyway, and her family wanted her to drop out of school by the time she was 16 to help raise her younger siblings.

I was tired of the fact that when I'd tried to bring sex education programs to my school—because there were students having sex as young as fourth grade and others who had ludicrous misconceptions about reproductive health (such as, "You can't get pregnant if it's a threesome")—I was told, "We don't have time for that." Well, I angrily wondered, *Who would make the time for those students graduating from eighth grade, only to come back to visit me the following year, pregnant in the ninth grade and no longer attending school?*

I was tired of seeing students come into school with dental problems so severe they would have multiple teeth rotting out of their mouths at once and in excruciating pain, which obviously stopped them from being able to learn in any significant way.

I was tired of spending my time gathering donated ties to teach my male students how to tie ties, knowing full well many of them would not make it through high school, let alone into college.

I was tired of seeing the poor students in Illinois receive 81 cents for every dollar spent on their wealthier counterparts, which meant low income students were missing out on valuable resources they needed and deserved as much as any more affluent Chicagoan students—everything from textbooks to access to technology, in order to be able to compete with their wealthier counterparts in a world that is increasingly dependent on technology. The two CPS schools where I worked were so under-resourced, I became accustomed to having to buy printer paper and even our own toilet paper.

Even more, I was outraged at discovering homicide is the leading cause of African American boys' deaths, and that in 2016 Chicago had more violent crime than New York City and Los Angeles combined, yet far too little was being done about it (CBS News, 2017).

I was deeply saddened knowing there enough homeless youth in Chicago every year to fill multiple football fields, and that only 54% of these youth over the age of 18 have completed high school (thenightministry.org). In addition, there have been, to date, no boarding schools established to serve these students.

I was saddened seeing some of my coworkers coming to school either physically ill, or mentally or emotionally so overwhelmed they could hardly function.

I hated knowing the Thompson principal worked around the clock but was continually berated by angry parents who were upset that their disobedient child had gotten suspended. And I hated finding out one day that a student had beaten her up so badly that after a few days at home recovering, she walked with a limp the rest of the year.

I hated knowing I'd gathered knitting supplies to teach some of my student groups how to knit (knowing how therapeutic it was), only to have those knitting supplies sit on the shelf gathering dust, because I got pulled into so many crises, they *rarely* got used—although my students loved to knit and were eager to learn.

None of this made me want to stop working with kids... but taken as a whole, it did make me want to leave CPS. However, as my vision evolved regarding how I could best help Chicago's inner city students, I came to realize there *was* a way I could serve them and effect change on a systemic, rather than a micro level. After being in CPS for seven years—which actually allowed me to be considered a "veteran" by CPS standards, as most social workers don't last that long—I planned both my departure from what I'd been doing and my arrival at a new strategy, one which I felt deeply inspired to begin implementing.

On the day I was determined to email my boss to tell her I wouldn't be coming back to school in the fall, I was walking along the lake, sobbing at the thought of leaving my students. All of a sudden, I looked up at the sky and saw a cloud formation that, to me, looked like a bird spreading its wings. I've never been one to see "messages" from nature, but in that moment it felt like a sign from the universe (maybe from Ryan), declaring I, too, needed to spread my wings.

TWENTY

• • •

Shortly after alerting my boss, I attended a conference in Portland called the World Domination Summit. Though the name sounds a bit bizarre, it was (and is still) a wonderful conference centered around the principles of community, adventure and service. The summit is led by Chris Guillebeau, a *New York Times* bestselling author who has visited all 196 countries of the world. On the second day at WDS, I was sitting in the balcony as one of the speakers, Michael Hyatt, took the stage. Michael shared with us that while he was putting together his talk, he'd spoken to an actuary who said that according to statistics, out of the audience of 2,000 people present at the summit, one of us would die within the next 30 days. His words hit me like a ton of bricks . . . and that moment changed everything for me. I instantly knew I could no longer wait until I was retired, or until "the right time," to begin building my dream.

Though I had a graduate degree in educational administration, I had not learned a single thing about how to build a school literally from the ground up—let alone how to start a boarding school. But I also realized, while it was true I didn't have a road-map to follow, no one else did, either. Even people who were more accomplished than I—the City of Chicago's mayor, or even the President of the United States—wouldn't have a clue. It had not been done before in Chicago, and there was no cheat sheet or *Dummy's Guide to Building a Boarding School* to assist me. But the fact that even President Obama wouldn't have immediately had the tools to do this somehow made me feel as if the playing field was level. I knew *he* would simply find the right people and the right resources to make it happen and figure it out along the way. I vowed to do the same.

EPILOGUE

• • •

The vision for Ryan Banks Academy began almost a decade ago. I instantly fell in love with the students and their families with whom I worked, but I also had a gut feeling there was something missing.

For 7 years, I'd counseled hundreds of students who regularly struggled with homelessness, hunger, violence, poverty, abuse or neglect. Clearly, there was no shortage of students who needed support on a regular basis to help them deal with the challenges outside the school environment that negatively impacted their ability to learn and achieve in the classroom. What I'd seen over and over for years was so many students in jeopardy of falling through the cracks, primarily because we could not provide them with the essential resources and support they needed to combat these external factors.

Thus, the vision for Ryan Banks Academy was born. There are literally tens of thousands of students in Chicago with immense potential who have a very slim chance of breaking through the vicious cycle of poverty without additional resources and support. Unfortunately, the current educational system is not effectively designed or sufficiently funded to provide these services. As former U.S. Secretary of Education Arne Duncan once said, "Even if we assume that, conservatively speaking, only 1% of Chicago students can benefit from a boarding school environment, that is still 4,000 students whose lives could be dramatically changed as a result of the chance to have such an opportunity."

Because until now Chicago has not had a boarding school to provide these opportunities, far too many students—indeed, thousands every year—never have the opportunity to build a bright future for themselves.

We know there is a dire need, and those who've helped develop and who are helping Ryan Banks Academy get off the ground are providing an innovative and proven solution. Boarding schools have existed for hundreds of years but are typically a privilege only accessible to the wealthy . . . and certainly not disadvantaged youth. Fortunately, more public boarding schools, such as the SEED model (where a whopping 92% of their graduates enroll in college) are popping up across the country and have achieved immeasurable success compared to their public school counterparts. The reason this occurs is not because the public schools aren't providing students with an education—it's because for these most vulnerable students, providing an education is simply not enough!

For students experiencing chronic homelessness, Ryan Banks Academy will provide them with stable housing, in order for them to be able to focus on their schoolwork. For students whose families struggle to put food on the table and who are used to coming to school hungry, we will supply nourishing meals, thereby allowing them to concentrate on their education, rather than the hunger pangs in their stomach. For students who have experienced trauma—whether from being a victim of or witness to violence in their home or in the neighborhood, or due to having lost a family member to gun violence or the prison system—we will provide them with regular and ongoing social and emotional support and counseling. Our goal is to equip them with the coping skills needed to process their trauma and grief and enable them to build healthy adaptation skills—as well as self-love and personal resilience—so necessary for those who've gone through events that can leave lifelong scars and wounds if not properly addressed.

Our students will benefit tremendously from the close-knit bonds that develop in a nurturing and accepting 24/7 environment. At Ryan Banks Academy, they will be able to build—perhaps for the first time in their lives—trusting relationships with their teachers, as well as with fellow classmates. Being surrounded by supportive and positive role models, they will develop the necessary habits to succeed academically, socially and professionally. For those students who've been trauma exposed and/or those who suffer from ADHD, our academic curriculum—based in large measure on experiential and expeditionary adventure learning—will allow students to engage in hands-on, projected-based learning that engages them in the learning process and taps into the strengths and passions of each individual.

At Ryan Banks Academy, since we can accelerate and reinforce student learning outside of traditional school hours, our students will graduate from high school with the academic and life skills needed to excel in college and in their professional careers. Coupled with our holistic educational model that addresses the needs of the whole child, our students will be given a firm foundation to help them escape poverty and enter into a college or vocation that can lead to much more positive and rewarding life outcomes. They will thereby be much better prepared to help transform their neighborhoods and the greater city of Chicago.

We invite you to be a part of this exciting new venture designed to transform young, underprivileged people's lives. Your support—whether it be your time or through a monetary donation—will allow us to ensure that talented, well-deserving students in inner-city Chicago have access to a safe and secure future.

Thank you for taking the time to learn more about Ryan Banks Academy and for your commitment to quality education. I would welcome the opportunity to address any questions you may have and look forward to hearing from you soon.

With gratitude,
Valerie Groth

ACKNOWLEDGEMENTS

• • •

I'm incredibly grateful to so many people who have not only helped make this book possible, but who have supported me along this journey and without whom, the Ryan Banks Academy initiative would not be possible. Writing this section proved to be incredibly challenging because I am indebted to not just a few but to hundreds of amazing individuals that I will feel forever thankful for including each and every one of Ryan Banks Academy's board members, advisors, and volunteers who have selfishly thrown so much of themselves into making RBA the best it can be. I can't thank you all by name, but please know how much I appreciate everyone who has been a part of this journey.

To Jim Paglia, I told you I would thank you first, and I meant it—there are no words to express my gratitude for your mentorship, support, and guidance over the years. If everyone had a mentor like you in their corner, the world would be a better place.

Special thanks goes to Ryan Lazarus, Sandee Kastrul, Dr. Kiley Russell, Jeff Bell, Jeff Garlin, Kendra Bostick, and Michael

Soguero. These fabulous human beings have contributed so much of their time, effort, and expertise to the project in various ways, and I don't believe Ryan Banks Academy would exist without them. If your name is listed in this paragraph, you're one of my heroes and I am thankful for you every day.

I'm also incredibly grateful to individuals who have come into my life at just the right times and thus, brought with you hope just when it was needed most: Deborah Liverett, Karen Goldfinger Baker, Will Rezin, Stacy Kolios, and Alicia Skruba.

Thank you to Ryan Banks for bringing so much joy into the lives of everyone who knew you in your twelve years on this planet, and to Ryan's aunt, Brigette, for being the motivation for me to do this work every day.

I'm also so grateful to all of my amazing friends for bringing so much laughter and joy into my life during good times and bad. Special thanks to Molly McGuigan and Steven Parry for being exceptionally supportive over the past year.

Thank you also to Willy Mathes, my editor, and to Colleen Keith, the graphic designer who designed this cover and for being so wonderful to work with.

Big thanks to all of my clients, whom I can't mention here by name but you know who you are and you inspire me every day to be a better person.

I'm also so grateful to the thousands of people in Chicago and across the nation who have supported our mission to build RBA.

My very deepest appreciation to my parents, Jon and Kathy, for instilling in me the belief that anything really *is* possible. And a huge thanks to my grandparents and sister, Laura—my amazing family is the reason I am doing this work.

And so, so many thanks to John, for your love, undying encouragement and support, and for believing in me even when I didn't believe in myself.

ABOUT THE AUTHOR

· · ·

Valerie Groth is a social innovator who is best known for inspiring possibility through her leadership as a nonprofit founder, executive coach, and internationally acclaimed speaker. She received her Bachelor's degree in Psychology from Indiana University, attended Dominican University where she received her Master's in Social Work, and received her second Master's degree in Educational Leadership from Concordia University.

Before starting her business as a coach and speaker, Val worked for many years as a school social worker in the inner city schools of Chicago. She worked with students in crisis, providing individual and group counseling services to students dealing with abuse, neglect, violence, hunger, and mental illness.

Valerie is now spearheading the mission to build Chicago's first boarding school for inner city students. Ryan Banks Academy (named after one of her former students who was lost to gun violence at the age of 12) seeks to impact the lives of students through a rigorous college and career preparatory education, a supportive boarding program, and a focus on personal development in a positive environment. Valerie has received national attention for her innovative work to transform the educational landscape for urban students.

In addition to her work as founder of Ryan Banks Academy, Valerie currently runs an executive life coaching practice at www. ValerieGroth.com coaching individuals who come to her from around the world. Valerie loves working with her clients on over-coming fear, gaining self-confidence, and making massive positive transformations in their life. She believes that everyone is capable of living an energized and impassioned life, and she loves to make the impossible POSSIBLE. She is also a sought after international speaker who is praised for her dynamic and innovative keynote presentations and for her contagious energy, enthusiasm, and ability to bring transformation to those in the audience.

ValerieGroth.com (http://valeriegroth.com/)*

RyanBanksAcademy.org (http://ryanbanksacademy.org/)

Instagram and Twitter: @ValerieGroth @RyanBanksChi

Facebook: facebook.com/RyanBanksChi (http://facebook. com/RyanBanksChi)

* For a free gift, articles, and updates,
sign up at http://valeriegroth.com/bookgift/